Praise for **The Dragons' Den Guide to Real-World Business Models**

"The case studies and practical examples in *The Dragons' Den Guide to Real-World Business Models* provide a no-nonsense approach to starting a business … a must-read for all burgeoning entrepreneurs."
    —Wendy Johannson, Co-Founder, Dig It, www.digithandwear.com

"The information on licensing is ideal for inventors interested in learning the steps one should take from idea to landing a successful licensing deal … easy to read and understand."
    —Chris Emery, Co-President, OMG's Candy, www.omgs.ca

"John Vyge's recommendations and detailed advice are helpful for both small and large businesses alike and delve into every facet of business development. Whether you are pondering a start-up, a pitch on *Dragons' Den* or your next business move, this is a must-read."
    —Andi Marcus, CEO, Mistura Beauty Solutions, www.misturabeauty.com

THE
DRAGONS' DEN
GUIDE TO
REAL-WORLD
BUSINESS
MODELS

THE PRODUCERS OF CBC'S DRAGONS' DEN WITH JOHN VYGE

WILEY

Library and Archives Canada Cataloguing in Publication Data

Vyge, John, 1966-
   The Dragons' den guide to real-world business models / John Vyge.

Includes index.
Issued also in electronic formats.
ISBN 978-1-118-66593-0

   1. Business planning. 2. New business enterprises—Computer networks.
3. Success in business. I. Title. II. Title: Guide to real-world business models.
III. Title: Real-world business models.

HD30.28.V946 2013   658.4'012   C2013-900901-9
ISBN: 9781118666029 (ebk); 9781118666005 (ebk); 9781118666081 (ebk)

Production Credits
Cover design: Ian Koo and
   Adrian So
Typesetting: Laserwords
Cover image: CBC --photographer
   Marayna Dickinson
Printer: Dickinson

Editorial Credits
Executive editor: Don Loney
Managing editor: Alison Maclean
Production editor: Pamela Vokey

John Wiley & Sons Canada, Ltd.
6045 Freemont Blvd.
Mississauga, Ontario
L5R 4J3

Printed in the United States

1 2 3 4 5 DP 17 16 15 14 13

Partner Credits
Sony Pictures Television:
Lindsay Pearl
   Director of Consumer Product
   Licensing
Lisa O' Connell
   Product & Brand Manager of
   Consumer Product Licensing

CBC Dragons' Den:
Karen Bower
Dianne Buckner
Molly Duignan
Sandra Kleinfeld
Keri Snider
Marc Thompson
Tracie Tighe

SONY
PICTURES
TELEVISION

TABLE OF CONTENTS

Foreword

By Doug Burgoyne, Founder and President, FROGBOX

Entrepreneurship is the lifeblood of a thriving economy. Perpetuating innovation and efficiency, entrepreneurship keeps incumbents on their toes and prevents economic stagnation.

Dragons' Den has become a cultural phenomenon, captivating the loyal viewership of millions of Canadians. Pitching your business to *any* investors can be exciting and terrifying—let alone pitching to five of the country's most successful venture capitalists. For those who have stepped up to that challenge, or plan to do so in the future, the Den is the opportunity of a lifetime.

John Vyge continues his outstanding series of books on how to pitch your business with *The Dragons' Den Guide to Real-World Business Models*. Presenting your pitch in a high-stress scenario can evoke strong emotional interference that runs the risk of damaging the overall integrity and effectiveness of the pitch. One of the biggest mistakes pitchers make is coming into the presentation from the inventor perspective rather than the business perspective. The inventor perspective focuses on the description and mechanics of the actual product or service itself. If you get hung up on these small details, you will be sure to hear Kevin interject, "Okay, but how will this make me money?" What Kevin is really asking is, "What is your business model?" Pitches often derail if you don't clearly and concisely answer this question. Vyge breaks down this question in a way that makes it easy for you to understand, and then prepare the best answer to help you receive an investment.

There are two parts to a successful pitch on *Dragons' Den:* the first involves getting some excitement going about your business and industry, and the second (and most important) involves being able to concisely communicate your business model. It is no accident that the Dragons have each achieved monumental levels of success. They are able to assess the long-term investment potential of a proposed venture. Therefore, providing a description of the product or service is essential; however, a well-structured description of the business model is your best tool with which to engage the interest of the Dragons.

The book also has a number of case studies surrounding successful real-life *Dragons' Den* pitches. One example that stands out is Marcus and Cam Dahl's pitch for Jet Pet Resort, their luxury airport pet resort. They built a full-scale dog suite in studio and furnished it with adorable puppies, instantly capturing the Dragons' attention. Soon after came the critical junction in the pitch: "We like your business. Now tell us about the business model." Luckily the Dahls were well prepared for the onslaught of questions about their business model and walked away with a deal. It is at these junctions where we often see pitches that began strong start to crash and burn. Vyge breaks down pitches like the Dahls' so you can understand how they made such a positive impact while others were chased out of the Den.

Since successfully pitching my business, FROGBOX, in Season 5, I have advised numerous pitchers to help prepare them for the show. One of the biggest hurdles is making your pitch concise. The Dragons have reviewed thousands of businesses in their careers and they don't have time for you to tell them all the details of your business. You have potentially spent every waking hour thinking about and working in your business for years, so to you every last detail holds importance. In the end, the most important detail that the Dragons want to hear is how you are going to make money.

If you want to maximize the possibility of making one or more of the Dragons (or any other venture capitalist) your partner, and minimize the chance of your pitch turning into a train wreck, I recommend two things: to watch every episode of *Dragons' Den* online and to read this book thoroughly. Vyge's book clearly outlines the important aspects of pitching, and reading it should be a requirement before stepping into the Den.

Take this advice, and when Kevin narrows his eyes and asks that pivotal question, you will be able to reply clearly and concisely: "Kevin, here is how we are going to get rich together."

Good luck!

Part I

Business Model Mechanics

Become familiar with the basic mechanics of business models. Assess your business opportunity to make sure that it is worth pursuing.

CHAPTER 1

WHAT DO YOU BRING TO THE TABLE?

"You are magic and that's what makes it worth looking at ... You are poised; you are professional. To have taken it as far as you have is very impressive. I'll make you an offer."

—Dragon to Pitcher

ASSESSMENT #1: Self-Assessment

Take an inventory of the financial, emotional, and physical sacrifices that you are willing to make to bring your business concept to the market. Launch your business concept with your eyes wide open, so that you are not shocked when the highest highs and lowest lows start to creep into your entrepreneurial psyche during the launch phase.

We have all seen the proverbial fish out of water, flapping back and forth. Pulled from the water where it happily thrives, it suffocates in its new environment. Many new entrepreneurs suffer the same initial shock when they leave a salaried or hourly position to enter the entrepreneurial world. The things you used to take for granted are no longer there: your computer breaks down, and you realize that you no longer have tech support to call; your printer mysteriously stops working, and the cash that you are lacking to fix it means you have to go into your meeting empty-handed; you're out of paper 30 minutes before you have to make that big proposal, and now you have to email it instead. The good news is that diverse backgrounds are precisely the reason so many entrepreneurs with sound business models succeed. Former corporate-world professionals understand immediately how to maintain a disciplined daily work schedule. Stay-at-home moms know how to multi-task and wear multiple hats. Hourly workers know how to get a job done within a limited amount of time and won't complain about working overtime.

If you want to eliminate having any fear whatsoever, embrace your past experiences—don't run from them. Know your limits, but don't be held back by them. Use every skill you have learned in the past to make your business happen. For example, pitcher Karlo Krauzig is trying to compete with the Absoluts, the Stolichnayas, and the Smirnoffs of the world. Do you know anyone who is launching a vodka brand? No, not likely. You need about $700,000 to $1 million to get up and running in the vodka business according to Krauzig, who came on the Den to seek funding for the Yukon Shine Distillery. The odds are stacked against you, especially in the high-stakes, highly competitive world of vodka distillation and distribution. But never underestimate the perseverance of an entrepreneur, especially if he's from the rugged Yukon where hard work is common and economic development grants are widely available.

YUKON SHINE DISTILLERY

Pitcher: Karlo Krauzig, Season 7, Episode 2

PRODUCT DESCRIPTION

Yukon Winter Vodka is unique because Karlo uses Yukon Gold potatoes, rye, barley, and even actual Yukon gold in his filtration process, and then bottles the vodka in a unique-looking premium bottle.

BACKGROUND

After he made his own fortune in real estate and the pet business, Karlo Krauzig decided to get into the vodka business. So, he spent the last five years learning everything he could about distilling and bottling vodka. He put $1 million of his own money into building a distillery to produce and bottle his "dangerously smooth" premium product. Then he came to the Den to secure funding and distribution connections so that he could launch his brand.

PROBLEM STATEMENT

How to compete in the high-margin, highly competitive vodka category.

BUSINESS MODEL

Karlo Krauzig built and owns a distillery that is capable of producing 50,000 bottles a year and will distribute them through BC Liquor Stores at a retail price of $50.

PROOF OF CONCEPT

- **Funding:** The Yukon offers several economic development grants that will support his launch.
- **Capacity:** Distillery is fully functional with the capacity to produce 50,000 bottles a year.
- **Distribution:** Landed a deal to distribute the vodka through BC Liquor Stores.

DRAGONS' DEAL

- **The Ask:** $300,000 for 33% equity.
- **Company Valuation:** $909,091.
- **The Deal:** $300,000 for 50% equity plus the distribution connections of one key Dragon.

THE WARM-UP: SELF-ASSESSMENT DEFINED

A **self-assessment** measures how fit you are to take on the business concept that you are proposing. The entrepreneurial world is not a meritocracy where hard work automatically pays off. It takes the right opportunity, good management, and a lot of luck. Entrepreneurs who succeed know as much about seeing an idea through to the end as when to quit. Overcommitting to a business idea that isn't going anywhere can be detrimental to your financial and emotional well-being. One way of staying on track is to conduct a self-assessment. The purpose of a self-assessment is to make sure you know exactly what you are getting yourself into personally when you decide to launch a new business concept.

Step 1: Personal Motivation—What inspired you to launch your business concept, and what will keep you inspired?

Inspiration

Many businesses are inspired by needs that entrepreneurs have in their business or personal worlds. When entrepreneurs fill those voids for themselves, they decide that others may want the same solutions. They then go out and build prototype products or services and begin the processes of launching their business concepts. When the obstacles and challenges of entrepreneurship unfold from there, it is important to stay connected to what originally inspired the launch of the business. But it is equally important to know what to do if your business isn't showing signs of earning back your investment and providing positive cash flow.

Role Modelling

One way to stay on track from day one is to use another successful business as a big-picture role model for what it is you're trying to do. That's not to say that you should follow a "me too" strategy by replicating a competitor's strategy. However, you can look at other industries to find companies that have used an approach that might work for your business. For example:

- *We want to do for financial advice what H&R Block did for tax preparation.*
- *I want to be the Martha Stewart of the personal chef industry.*
- *We want to do for soup what Mr. Sub did for sandwiches.*
- *We want to do for chicken what Boston Pizza did for pizza.*

Outcomes

Outcomes are what you want both financially and emotionally in return for launching your business concept in the first place. It is critical that you set clear personal outcomes for your business so that pride doesn't keep you committed to a business that isn't going anywhere. For example:

- **Short-Term Goals (One Year):** What would have to happen in the next 12 months for you to feel successful? *Example: Generate enough income from my business to pay for my basic living expenses and not go into personal debt.*
- **Medium-Term Goals (Two to Three Years):** What would have to happen in the next two to three years for you to feel successful? *Example: Hire a business manager so that I can stay focused on developing the best business systems, and have more time with my family.*
- **Long-Term Goals (Five+ Years):** What would have to happen in the next five+ years for you to feel successful? *Example: Sell my business for two to three times annual sales within five years.*

Step 2: Personal Inventory—What experience and expertise do you bring to the table?

Prior experience in your industry can give you access to contacts, resources, and efficiencies that your competitors may lack. At the same time, being a domain expert in your industry can be extraordinarily helpful when launching a new product or service because you won't have a learning curve to overcome. Your efforts can be focused more on action than on finding your way. And if, instead, you're a generalist or jack of all trades, you will find your diverse skills suddenly come to life when you go to launch a new business concept. Skills fall into one of two categories:

- **Soft Skills:** Non-technical skills, such as how to sell, how to develop rapport, or how to work a room.
- **Hard Skills:** Technical skills, such as how to produce PowerPoint presentations, how to make your product, or how to perform a specific service.

Step 3: Personal Resources—What amount of time and money are you able to commit?

Time Resources

A business has a strange way of taking over your psyche. That's because you are now the boss and you're responsible for everything that goes on. But even if you are highly dedicated to your business idea and want to sacrifice everything to make it succeed, you won't be giving your business everything it needs if your personal world falls apart around you. Be sure to structure your day to include family time, work time, and personal time so you can counterbalance the psychological demands of growing a business. Also, have a clear vision of the type of business you are seeking to develop. Here are some guidelines (not hard-and-fast rules) to consider:

- **Hobby Business (10 Hours/Week):** A part-time business designed to supplement income from another line of work.
- **Lifestyle Business (40+ Hours/Week):** A full-time business designed to provide an annual salary that supports your family's lifestyle.
- **Growth Business (60 to 80 Hours/Week):** A full-time business designed to provide an annual salary plus a future liquidity event that can make you a very rich entrepreneur.

Financial Resources

Launching a new business concept is not an all-or-nothing process. Although it is certainly your prerogative to leverage your home, cash out your retirement plan, and max out your credit cards, treat such actions with extreme caution. For every person who wins by betting the farm, there are countless others who have destroyed their lives. The wisest course of action might be to launch your business concept while you are still working. One way of controlling the financial risk you take is to structure your personal finances into wealth "buckets," like those shown below. A wealth bucket is a dollar amount of money that you set aside for a specific funding goal. Then set limits on how much of each of those buckets you are able to sacrifice without putting your family at risk. These wealth buckets include:

- **Living Expenses:** Cut all discretionary expenses out of your budget while you are not drawing a salary.
- **Emergency Fund:** Set aside 6 to 12 months' worth of living expenses before you commit full time to your business, if possible. Consider exiting the business once you burn through your emergency funds. Be cautious about taking on an external debt load, be it from family members or arm's-length investors.
- **Major Assets:** Put off major expenses—such as the purchase of a car or house, or taking a vacation—until your business is generating free cash flow to pay you a salary. As a general guideline, don't tap into the equity of your major assets to fund your business.
- **Education Funds:** Don't raid your children's college education fund while you are starting your business.
- **Retirement Funds:** Set aside 15% of any salary you do draw from your business. As a general guideline, don't tap into your retirement accounts to fund your business.
- **Net Worth**: Try not to risk more than 5% to 15% of your total net worth on your business. Use outside capital sources or exit the business once you reach the upper end of this threshold.

These too are guidelines, not hard-and-fast rules. There are many people who have risked it all and succeeded, but they are few and far between. These guidelines are here for the rest of us and can help keep you financially solvent. You should also seek advice from an accountant who has experience with entrepreneurs.

Step 4: Personality Type—What personality traits do you bring to the table?
Entrepreneurs don't have the luxury of typecasting themselves based on past behaviour. The most successful entrepreneurs adapt to their new surroundings by modifying past work styles, problem-solving approaches, and levels of risk tolerance. The key to adapting to new market opportunities as they present themselves is to know yourself in advance, so you can get out of your own way.

Work Style
Your job as an entrepreneur is to get things done, not necessarily to do things yourself. It is important to understand your own personal work style so that you understand your own built-in limitations.

- **Delegators:** Delegators get things done through other people. They save valuable time by getting others to do their work. The downside of being a delegator is that you can burn through *financial* resources very quickly if you pay others to do everything.
- **Do-It-Yourselfers:** Do-it-yourselfers like the personal challenge of doing everything themselves. They conserve cash by doing everything in-house. The downside of being a do-it-yourselfer is that valuable *time* resources are often wasted on low-value projects.
- **Collaborators:** Collaborators work well with others and put the outcome of their work above themselves. They conserve both time and financial resources by leveraging strategic relationships with others to achieve an overriding goal. The downside of being a collaborator is that you have to check your ego at the door because you end up having to share the accolades that go with a successful outcome.

Problem-Solving Approach
Entrepreneurs run into brick walls all the time. However, the most successful ones deal with problems head-on so that they can move on to bigger and better things. How you deal with problems as they arise can determine whether your business survives or fails. There are two approaches:

- **Problem Solver:** Entrepreneurs who take this approach to problems deal with thorny situations head-on. If you are a problem solver, make sure you don't get sidetracked putting out fires all day. Systemize your business processes to reduce the number of problems that occur.

- **Problem Avoider:** Entrepreneurs who take this approach to problems avoid thorny situations like the plague and sometimes just ignore them. Not recommended. If you are a problem avoider, make sure you have someone on your support team on speed dial to call if you run into an unexpected challenge.

Risk Tolerance

When you sign a hypothetical contract to become an entrepreneur, you are agreeing to seek profit at the risk of loss. Risk is a big part of the game. Take too much risk and you might end up penniless. Take too little risk and you might not capitalize on the one and only opportunity you have to make your business concept fly. Part of dealing with risk is understanding your personal tolerance for it.

- **Risk Taker:** Entrepreneurs who take this approach to risk often see opportunity everywhere. They are prone to betting the farm on ideas that may have no basis in reality.
- **Risk Manager:** Entrepreneurs who take this approach to risk weigh the costs and benefits of each decision to be made. The downside of being a risk manager is that you can start to see risk in everything. You might miss a valuable opportunity because you can't make a decision quickly enough.

Step 5: Barriers—What will you do when you hit a brick wall?

Most business problems are never as bad as they seem. One way to deal with business problems is called **root-cause analysis.** Root-cause analysis is at the heart of many Lean Six Sigma efforts at highly efficient organizations such as Dell, Toyota, and Intel. Essentially, you start with a problem and dig deeper to get to the cause behind it by asking questions about the problem. Then you make the required changes based on your conclusions about the initial problem.

5 Whys

One deceptively simple problem-solving concept used at the Toyota Motor Corporation is the 5 Whys.[1] It is such a simple concept that you can apply it to just about any problem in order to discover a solution to that problem. Here are two self-explanatory examples:

PROBLEM: My Business Is Starving for Cash

- Why? Because our customers don't pay up front.
- Why? Because we don't ask them to.
- Why? Because we offer flexible payment terms.
- Why? Because we think customers won't pay us up front.
- Why? Because one of our first customers asked us if he could have payment terms and we haven't changed the policy since.

Solution: From these five responses you might conclude that very few customers actually request payment terms and that you should stop offering them. By not offering them, you may be able to resolve your cash-flow issue almost immediately.

PROBLEM: I Don't Spend Enough Time with My Family

- Why? Because I wear many hats in my business.
- Why? Because I don't have enough staff.
- Why? Because I can't train people to do my job.
- Why? Because I don't have a how-to manual for roles in my business.
- Why? Because I haven't taken the time to make one.

Solution: From these five responses you might conclude that you are taking on too many roles in your business. It might be time to create an operating manual for each area of your business so you can hire staff to do some of the things you shouldn't be doing yourself.

Support Circle

Bringing a sound business concept to market requires an unwavering commitment to your vision. A support circle you can turn to any time you have a challenge or need feedback can be one of the most critical resources you have. There are three types of support that any entrepreneur with a new business idea can set up for low or no cost:

- **Family and Friends:** Family and friends can be the best and worst type of support for your business. Supportive family members can bring you out of a tailspin when one obstacle after another presents itself. At the same time, they can also be the ones who tell you to trudge forward and pursue an idea that really has no hope of succeeding in the marketplace.
- **Advisory Board:** A formal or informal advisory board can help you ride out the highs and lows of your business. A seemingly insurmountable obstacle can usually be overcome after a quick chat with someone on your advisory board who has been in a similar position before.
- **Business Coach:** A business coach can make you accountable at weekly or monthly checkpoints to the short-, medium-, and long-term outcomes you've set in advance.

Step 6: Personal Boundaries—Knowing when to say when

Business is about money, not personal ego. Putting your entire life at risk for an idea that has no long-term merit is bad business and could prevent you from finding one that does have merit. For every entrepreneur who bet his or her home, retirement, and family life for an idea and won big, there are many others whose lives were ruined by a business idea that got out of control. This is not to say that you shouldn't take the risk or that you can keep any of this from happening. Just be sure to set your personal limits so you know when to bring outsiders in or when to exit the business. Consider your:

- **Financial Limits:** What is the greatest amount of personal capital that you are able to invest without putting your family at risk? Maybe $10,000 is what you can afford, and after that, you need to look for outside investors.
- **Time Limits:** What amount of time are you able to invest daily and over the long term without destroying your family life? You might decide that you will give yourself three years, at which point you will consider exiting the business or bringing in outsiders if your goals are not being met.
- **Emotional Limits:** What amount of energy are you able to invest without destroying your health? This is also tied to your risk profile: take on more risk than your system can handle and you may take on too much stress.

DRAGON LORE

Any time someone tells you that you have a ridiculous idea, remember the Banana Guard, which sold 700,000 units before its inventors appeared on *Dragons' Den.* Test and prove your idea, and don't let the skeptics derail you if your business plan has a solid foundation.

By knowing what you bring to the table, you'll be far more likely to choose a path that fits your abilities. For example, having a history as a yoga instructor certainly comes in handy when you try to launch a line of healthy beverages. You will certainly know your customer. And a yoga background will also help you stay calm under pressure, if you are fortunate enough to get in front of professional investors like the Dragons.

TONICA KOMBUCHA

Pitcher: Zoey Shamai, Season 7, Episode 8

PRODUCT DESCRIPTION

A beverage based on an ancient tonic called Kombucha, which is said to aid digestion.

BACKGROUND

Zoey Shamai is a yoga instructor who produces a beverage line called Tonica Kombucha. She says that "80% of the immune system resides in the gut so if you have a healthy belly, you have a healthy body." She would like to use the funds to upgrade her facilities and fund future marketing efforts.

PROBLEM STATEMENT

How to help the immune system by improving digestion.

BUSINESS MODEL

Produces and sells cases of Tonica Kombucha through over 200 stores across Canada. The production cost per case of 12 is $8.86, or $0.74 a bottle. Each bottle retails at $3.99 and yields a 71% profit margin to Tonica. Shamai's product is the only one that flavours with teas and has natural carbonation.

PROOF OF CONCEPT

- **Revenue:** $135,000 in sales last year and projected sales of $303,000 this year.
- **Distribution:** Retails through 200 stores across Canada.

DRAGONS' DEAL

- **The Ask:** $125,000 for 25% of the company.
- **Company Valuation:** $500,000.
- **The Deal:** $125,000 for 25% of the company, with a 50% vote in the business.

START-UP ESSENTIALS: How to Conduct a Self-Assessment

Take a personal inventory of your resources and the sacrifices you are willing to make to bring your business concept to the marketplace. This self-assessment is more about understanding your limits than it is about setting them. When you understand your limits, you'll be in a better position to objectively weigh the costs against the benefits of important business decisions.

Step 1: Personal Motivation—What inspired you to launch your business concept, and what will keep you inspired?

- ❑ **Original Inspiration:** What inspired you to launch your business concept? *Example: I couldn't find the resources I needed to teach my students effectively.*
- ❑ **Role Model:** What real-world business success would you like to be similar to? *Example: Atomic Tea wants to be the Starbucks of tea.*
- ❑ **Outcomes:** What do you want out of your business? *Example: My exit strategy is to sell my business in five years.*

Step 2: Personal Inventory—What experience and expertise do you bring to the table?

Expertise: What relevant skills do you bring to the table?

- ❑ **Hard Skills:** What relevant hard (technical) skills do you bring to the table? *Examples: Product design, computer programming, knitting, gourmet cooking.*
- ❑ **Soft Skills:** What relevant soft (non-technical) skills do you bring to the table? *Examples: People skills, sales, negotiating.*

Experience: What experience do you have in this type of business? Are you a domain expert in this industry or a jack of all trades with transferable skills that work in any industry?

❑ **Domain Expert:** Build a support team around you to handle those tasks that you are not good at.

❑ **Jack of All Trades:** Clearly define your highest and best use so you don't waste time on tasks that would be better done by someone else.

Step 3: Personal Resources—What amount of time and money are you able to commit?

Time Resources: What amount of time daily are you ready, willing, and able to commit to launching your business concept?

❑ Full time (eight hours or more per day)

❑ Part time (four hours or less per day)

❑ Hobby time (ten hours per week)

Financial Resources: What amounts of money are you going to assign to each wealth bucket?

Do you have an alternative source of income or a reserve amount of cash set aside for living expenses, to support yourself financially during the first 6 to 24 months of launching your business concept?

❑ Yes

❑ No

Do you have assets to fall back on if this business doesn't work?

❑ Yes

❑ No

Step 4: Personality Type—What personality traits do you bring to the table?

Work Style: How do you complete tasks and projects?

❑ Delegator

❑ Do-it-yourselfer

❑ Collaborator

Problem-Solving Approach: How do you react to sudden challenges and obstacles?

❑ Problem solver

❑ Problem avoider

Risk Tolerance: How do you handle risk?

❑ Risk taker

❑ Risk manager

Step 5: Barriers—What will you do when you hit a brick wall?

Support Circle: Everyone needs someone to "talk them off the ledge" once in a while. Who will act as your emotional support when you are faced with seemingly insurmountable challenges?

❑ Friend (name one)

❑ Family member (name one)

❑ Business coach (name one)

❑ Advisory board (name one)

Step 6: Personal Boundaries—Knowing when to say when

Time Limit: What amount of time do you give yourself to make your business work?

❑ One year (*Example: Then I go back to work*)

❑ Three years (*Example: Then I partner with someone else*)

❑ Five years (*Example: Then I liquidate the business*)

Financial Limit: What amount of capital will you personally limit yourself to committing to?

❑ Up to $10,000

❑ Up to $100,000

❑ Up to $1,000,000

❑ Other

Emotional Limit: Why do you want to be in this business? Are you physically prepared for the stresses that come with bringing a business concept to market? Is your family prepared for the amount of time and energy your business is going to take?

Starting and running a business can take you through higher highs and lower lows than you've ever experienced in your life. Hopefully this chapter has made you more aware of your strengths and weaknesses so that you can manage them better. It's now time to summarize why you feel that your business will succeed using the one-page business case format that you'll follow in the next chapter.

CHAPTER 2

WHY WILL YOUR BUSINESS SUCCEED?

"I have no problem with what you're doing at all. You're a legitimate businessman, you're pursuing an opportunity, and you're servicing a need that people have … Good luck to you, and run a good business."

—Dragon to Pitcher

ASSESSMENT #2: The One-Page Business Case

Complete a hypothetical summary of why your business concept is justified. This summary should describe your overall vision and financial justification for your business concept. It is not intended to be a multi-day research project. Just two to three hours of brainstorming should suffice.

A new business idea is like a science fair project. You start out with a hypothesis describing what will happen if you pursue your business concept. You map out your idea in your head or on paper, and then you set up an environment where you can conduct a series of tests to prove that your hypothesis is true. These tests start with a simple prototype product or service and a hypothesis that it can solve a real problem. You then move to a pilot-test stage, where you look for proof not only that your concept works but also that people will actually pay you for it. And finally, you conduct a full-scale feasibility study to make sure your business concept has market, technical, and financial feasibility on a larger scale. If your idea passes your feasibility study with flying colours, you build a business plan around it, and you commit larger amounts of your own capital or investors' capital to the project. By this point, your business has been well thought out. The starting point for your business equivalent of a science project is called a **one-page business case**.

And if you are fortunate enough to make it onto *Dragons' Den*, your one-page business case could prove to be the most valuable piece of your pitch. When pitchers Natasha Vandenhurk and Elysia Vandenhurk visited the Dragons' Den, they had a farm-grown passion for their business and a willingness to work hard until they succeeded. They calmly described the history of their business, laid out the business case for their idea, and left with a deal in hand.

THREE FARMERS CAMELINA OIL

Pitchers: Natasha Vandenhurk and Elysia Vandenhurk, Season 7, Episode 4

PRODUCT DESCRIPTION

A line of healthy oils made from an ancient seed called camelina.

BACKGROUND

Three neighbouring farmers were introduced to a nutritionally dense seed called camelina sativa that originated in parts of Northern Europe. Two daughters of one of the farmers, Natasha and Elysia Vandenhurk, saw the benefits of this ancient grain and partnered with a Red Seal chef to produce cold-press oil from the seed in Saskatchewan, Canada. Because this ancient grain is rich in omega-3 fatty acids, it can be used for healthy cooking oil, dips, and marinades.

PROBLEM STATEMENT

Omega-3s are very hard to source in a diet because you can only get them in fish and certain plant sources.

BUSINESS MODEL

Three Farmers camelina oil, which is rich in omega-3s, is produced by the company in Saskatchewan and sold through independent grocery stores throughout Canada at a retail price of $25 per bottle.

PROOF OF CONCEPT

- **Revenue:** Projecting $250,000 in sales this year.
- **Growth:** Projecting 300% growth over last year.
- **Distribution:** Sells directly to retailers.

DRAGONS' DEAL

- **The Ask:** $150,000 for 18% equity.
- **Company Valuation:** $833,000.
- **The Deal:** $150,000 for 20% equity from a strategic investor who brings marketing and distribution expertise.

THE WARM-UP: BUSINESS CASE DEFINED

A **business case** is the business equivalent of a hypothesis. It is a one-page summary of the reasons why you expect that your product, service, or business concept is financially justified. The purpose of a one-page business case is to help you weed out a not-so-clever business idea before it gets out of hand—financially or time-wise. The process of writing a business case typically involves two to three hours of brainstorming on the following:

- **Background:** What was the inspiration behind this business?
- **Problem Statement:** What problem does your business solve?
- **Current Alternatives:** How does the customer currently solve the problem?
- **Proposed Product or Service:** How does your product or service work?
- **Business Case:** What is the financial justification for your business?

Business Case: Why Do You Feel That You Have a Winning Business Idea?

A business can turn your entire world upside down. Once you become gripped by it and the financial potential it has for your life, you start to develop tunnel vision. Pretty soon your family, friends, and colleagues become less of a priority, and your business starts to take on a life of its own. It is imperative that you map out the reasons why your business is financially justified before you take the leap.

One-Page Summary

This process starts with a quick, back-of-the-napkin-type summary of your business idea—your business case. You could certainly produce a 20-page document, but for your purposes here, you need a one-page summary, because at this stage the business idea is only a hypothesis. A business case shouldn't be confused with a feasibility study or pilot test, which are real-world tests of your business idea. Rather, a business case is the outcome of two to three hours of brainstorming your business idea over a glass of wine, a coffee, or a tea cooler from Atomic Tea (a previous visitor to the Dragons' Den).

Stakeholders

There will be many stakeholders who will depend on you to make a sound business decision, so it's important to summarize your business idea succinctly. A business should not be started unless it supports the needs of various stakeholders involved in your business. People with something at stake include customers, who will be parting with their hard-earned money to pay you for a product or service that they hope will solve their problem. They include investors, who invest in your business idea in exchange for a reasonable return on investment (ROI). They include company founders (you, and your partners if you have any), who will need the business to meet their own financial requirements, including their salary needs and future profit potential.

Guidelines

A business case is not a full-blown research project. If it takes you more than two or three hours to summarize your hypothesis, then you might have to rethink your idea. Here are some simple guidelines:

- Keep your answers to the questions posed above (in the opening of "The Warm-Up: Business Case Defined" section) to one sentence.
- Keep the entire business case to one page.
- Keep your business case to general assumptions. Do not include detailed research.
- Treat the business case like a scientific hypothesis, not a full-blown research project.

DRAGON LORE

If you want to shorten your go-to-market cycle, emulate business role models that have already achieved in their industry what you are trying to achieve in yours.

Entrepreneurs who wrap sound business models around their product ideas are more likely to succeed with investors than the ones who just show up with a product. When Teach My Toddler founder Christy Cook visited the Dragons' Den back in Season 3 with her line of teaching tool kits for toddlers and babies, she knew she had something special. And though she was unable to convince the Dragons to make a deal on the spot, she left with a promise. If she could prove her business model, she would have an open door to a key Dragon in the near future.

TEACH MY TODDLER

Pitcher: Christy Cook, Season 3, Episode 6

PRODUCT DESCRIPTION

A learning kit with 17 teaching tools that teaches toddlers about the alphabet, shapes, colours, and numbers.

BACKGROUND

Christy Cook writes books for toddlers and packages them in kits. She came to the Den to secure growth capital to expand into the United States and across Canada.

PROBLEM STATEMENT

How to teach your toddler to read.

BUSINESS MODEL

Pitcher Christy Cook plans to sell her learning tools through toy stores, baby stores, and bookstores across Canada and the United States. She produces, packages, and markets her learning kits herself and each kit includes books, posters, puzzles, and flashcards.

PROOF OF CONCEPT

- **Revenue:** 500 units sold in six months.

DRAGONS' DEAL

- **The Ask:** $100,000 for 20% equity.
- **Company Valuation:** $500,000.
- **The Deal:** $0.

START-UP ESSENTIALS: How to Create a One-Page Business Case

Pretend you are a lawyer in a courtroom with limited time to convince a jury of friends, family, customers, and suppliers that there are real financial and non-financial needs for the product or service you plan to launch. Summarize the overriding reasons why you think that you have a winning business concept.

1. BACKGROUND

Describe the original inspiration for your business concept.

Example: I started noticing an increase in the number of newspaper stories about potential links between electronic devices in the home and cancer. While electronics manufacturers continue to present "proof" that there is no link, the fact that cigarette manufacturers said the same thing—that they didn't see a link between smoking and cancer either—scared me to death. So I decided to build a prototype solution called, with deliberate irony, "The Kill Switch."

2. PROBLEM STATEMENT

Define the problem that your product or service solves or how your product or service improves upon a current alternative in the marketplace.

Example: All of the electronic devices in our homes are exposing us to an enormous amount of radiation while we sleep. This radiation is being linked to a noticeable increase in cancer over the last 50 years.

3. PROPOSED PRODUCT OR SERVICE

In two to three sentences, discuss what your product or service is and how it works. Think in terms of its functional use, its cost-cutting ability, and its ability to increase revenue (if it's a product or service that other businesses will buy from you).

Example: The Kill Switch is a button you put on your wall that powers down all of your electronics wirelessly. It comes with a set of attachments that you put in each of the wall sockets that you use to power your computers, iPods, cellphones, and television sets. It also comes with a software app so that your computers and cellphones can be shut down first, before the power is cut. It can even be programmed to shut itself off at night, and power down and power up your electronics on a timed schedule.

4. BUSINESS CASE (FINANCIAL JUSTIFICATION)

The heart of the business case is the financial justification for your product, service, or business.

- Reason 1 (Revenue Model).
  Example: Electrical product manufacturers pay us a royalty fee for the use of our trademark and business systems.

- Reason 2 (Revenue Target/Revenue to Date/Users to Date).
  Example: $450,000 in the last 12 months.

- Reason 3 (Profit Potential).
  Example: 30% profit margin.

- Reason 4 (Projected ROI).
  Example: Ten times initial investment within five years.

- Reason 5 (Start-Up Funds Required).
  Example: $300,000.

- Reason 6 (Proof of Concept).
  Example: Prototypes tested, awards received, customers to date, revenue to date.

5. CONCLUSION

Summarize in one sentence the overriding justification for your product or service. What is the financial justification for your business concept? What is the non-financial justification for your business concept? What personal mission are you on?

Example: We just signed a licensing deal with a global electronics company to manufacture and distribute 50,000 units for a fee.

A one-page business case is one more step in the process of formalizing your rationale for your business, so that you don't overcommit to a weak business idea. Now that you have completed a hypothetical summary of why your business is justified, it's time to take another step in the feasibility study process by testing it using the real-world feasibility study process in the next chapter. This is where you dip your foot in the market to gauge its temperature—before you dive in head-first.

CHAPTER 3

IS YOUR IDEA TECHNICALLY AND FINANCIALLY FEASIBLE?

"The fact that you have thought this through the way you have is so admirable. You're filling a market niche that's very interesting to me. A mom is too busy to go out and get all the pieces. A mom is too busy to think about how she's going to put this all together."

—Dragon to Pitcher

ASSESSMENT #3: Feasibility Study

Complete an analysis of the commercial viability of your business concept. This analysis should be completed before you write your business plan, and may deem your business plan unnecessary if the outcome is that your business won't work.

Every business needs a kill switch, something to shut it off before it gets out of hand if it's simply not going to work. In business, that kill switch is the **feasibility study.** A properly conducted feasibility study should test for market, technical, and financial feasibility before you write your business plan. You can't move forward with your business idea just because it appears to solve a problem or because your spouse loves it. The feasibility study is the litmus test for determining if your business is a go or a no-go. If you want scalable growth in revenue, put your concept through a feasibility study before you go any further.

And the first step in any feasibility study is technical feasibility. Can you produce a working, commercial version of your product or service? It's one thing to create a prototype product in a lab or in a garage. It's another to be able to produce it in a high enough volume that satisfies the needs of the market. So when pitchers Bill Redelmeier and Robert Egli from

Bioflavia came to the Dragons' Den with a market-ready version of their product, and a production process in place, the Dragons were much more amenable to a deal.

BIOFLAVIA

Pitchers: Bill Redelmeier and Robert Egli, Season 6, Episode 18

PRODUCT DESCRIPTION

Bioflavia is a powdered grape-skin product that is an ingredient for companies that make sauces, smoothie drinks, and baked goods.

BACKGROUND

Pitcher Bill Redelmeier and his wife own Southbrook Winery, the first winery in Canada to achieve the Gold level of LEED (Leadership in Energy and Environmental Design) certification. Their ongoing effort to be "as sustainable as possible" led them to come up with a way to make use of the byproduct of the red wine–making process—pomace.

PROBLEM STATEMENT

When you make red wine, 25% of what is left over is waste called "pomace," which is made up of flavonoid-rich skin seeds.

BUSINESS MODEL

The company converts grape skin pomace from their own vineyard and other wineries into a powdered product called "Bioflavia." The product is sold as an ingredient to manufacturers and to consumers at a 50% margin.

PROOF OF CONCEPT

- **Revenue:** $20,000 in sales in four weeks and purchase orders in hand for $125,000.

DRAGONS' DEAL

- **The Ask:** $100,000 for 15% equity.
- **Company Valuation:** $666,666.
- **The Deal:** $100,000 for 35% equity.

THE WARM-UP: FEASIBILITY STUDY DEFINED

Until now, you've been in the pre-feasibility stage figuring out what needs to be incorporated in your product or service launch to be successful. Now it's time for a full-scale go/no-go assessment of your business idea. The purpose of a **feasibility study** is to weed out the make-or-break issues that could help or hinder your business concept. The process of conducting a feasibility study involves:

- **Market Feasibility Testing:** Is the market large enough to support your business goals?
- **Technical Feasibility Testing:** Does your product or service work as promised, and can it be produced at the volume scale that is required to support your business goals?
- **Financial Feasibility Testing:** Are your potential revenue and profit enough to support your business goals?

The Feasibility Study

A feasibility study is a written summary of the key aspects of your business that provide support for your business model. As a general guideline, try to keep it to two pages, though some studies are as short as one page, or as long as (or longer than) full-scale business plans. Writing a feasibility study involves the process of thinking through a business idea and documenting it on paper. Its purpose is to determine the market, technical, and financial feasibility of your business. It is not a business plan; it is a precursor to a business plan. It serves as a pre-business-planning checkpoint to help you make a final go/no-go decision on your business model. If you decide to move forward with your business, the research yielded by the process is included in the business plan, a planning document that helps delineate what actions need to be taken in order to capitalize on your market opportunity.

The Market Feasibility of Your Concept

The key to estimating the demand for your product or service is to make your estimates realistic. Crazy market-share predictions are meaningless if you can't trace them back to actual steps that you will take to make them happen. Here are the core components of market-size analysis.

- **Total Available Market (TAM):** The total industry-wide market for your product or service in a year.
- **Serviceable Available Market (SAM):** The portion of the TAM that could conceivably buy your category of product or service.

- **Serviceable Obtainable Market (SOM):** The share of the SAM you could conceivably capture.
- **Compound Annual Growth Rate:** The historical growth rate of your market.

The Technical Feasibility of Your Concept

Technical feasibility is a screening framework that helps you assess whether your product or service can be delivered in a timely manner. The purpose of the process is to demonstrate that you will be capable of producing a fully functional, market-ready product or service, in real-world conditions, when customers are waiting. When you list the components of your product or the tangible components of your service, consider trade-offs that are possible if some of the components prove to be cost-prohibitive.

What Technical Resources Are Required?

A business needs an endless flow of resources to build its products or deliver its services. Breaking down your offering into its component parts will not only help you assess your capabilities but also enable you to put a cost on each component later. When testing whether your product or service can be delivered as promised, consider these resource needs:

- **Know-How:** The methodology required to produce your product or service.
- **Labour:** The level of skill required.
- **Raw Materials:** The type of inputs required.
- **Equipment:** The type of equipment and technology required.
- **Other Inputs:** Any other miscellaneous resources required.

What Are the Technical Constraints?

When you produce a product or perform a service in a testing environment, time is not an issue because a customer is not waiting. However, once you go to market, time becomes a major issue. A customer won't care how good your product or service is if you can't deliver it when it's needed. When considering your technical feasibility, keep the following in mind:

- **Time Constraints:** Will you be able to deliver your products and services when your customers want them?
- **Location Constraints:** Will your environment enable you to deliver your offering in an efficient manner?

The Financial Feasibility of Your Concept

Financial feasibility is a screening framework for your business concept that helps you assess whether you can turn a profit on each product or service unit sold, and if you can operate your overall business at a profit. The purpose of conducting a financial feasibility study is to make sure that your expected revenues will exceed your expected costs (including your required return on your business). Of course, at this point you might want to call the accountant in the family to help you put together your estimates, but here are the basics.

Revenue Estimate

Revenue estimates should be realistic, not pie-in-the-sky. A financial feasibility study is not a sales pitch that you are using to convince others that your business will be successful. These numbers are here to give you a realistic set of expectations of the success potential of your business idea.

Revenue Formula

The background behind the components of this formula will vary depending on what you sell. Your definition of what a unit is might be an hour of time, one product, or a service contract. But the core formula itself should stay the same:

$$\text{Revenue Estimate} = \text{Estimated Units Sold} \times \text{Price of Each Unit}$$

Costs to Run Your Business

Two of the main categories of costs that you need to watch for in your business, assuming you don't have any debt-financing costs, are:

- **Cost of Goods Sold**: Estimated units sold multiplied by cost per unit of product or service sold (e.g., cost of resale goods, costs of raw materials for products produced, cost of labour performed).
- **Selling, General, and Administrative Expenses:** Estimated costs to market and sell your product or service plus the costs required to run your business (e.g., rent, utilities, office salaries, office supplies, insurance, licenses).

Profitability of Your Business

The two areas of your business that determine profitability are your costs of goods sold and your costs of overall operation. The two measures that you must take are gross profits (revenues from sales, less cost of goods sold) and operating profits (which net out your expenses like rent, administration, and marketing). If your gross profits are in the black but your operating expenses are too high and trigger a loss, then ultimately your business will need to be shut down. Throwing money at it to keep it afloat is like throwing money to the wind.

Gross Profit Formula (Product Profit)
This is the profit of your business before selling, general, and administrative expenses are reflected:

$$\text{Gross Profit} = \text{Revenue} - \text{Cost of Goods Sold}$$

Operating Profit Formula
This is the pre-tax and pre-interest profit of your business:

$$\text{Operating Profit} = \text{Gross Profit} - \text{Selling, General, and Administrative Expenses}$$

DRAGON LORE

Sometimes the best feasibility study is to just get your product or service out into the hands of real paying customers.

When the pitchers behind Urban Vendor visited the Dragons' Den, they had already proven the technical feasibility of their vending machine business. Vending machine technology is widely available, so proving that it worked with healthy products would not be enough to impress a Dragon. So the two students from Antigonish took a different tack and tried to convince the Dragons that they had a financially feasible business that was ready for an investment.

URBAN VENDOR

Pitchers: A.J. MacQuarrie and Christina Wilson, Season 6, Episode 13

PRODUCT DESCRIPTION

A green-friendly vending machine that provides an alternative to traditional junk food vending machines.

BACKGROUND

Two full-time students from Nova Scotia have found an idea that they think will disrupt the vending machine industry. The pitchers have managed to establish distribution locations for their vending machines, while only working on the business part time.

PROBLEM STATEMENT

Convenient good health food is hard to find.

BUSINESS MODEL

A vending machine that contains healthier versions of what you'd find in a traditional vending machine. The company earns a gross profit margin of $1 per item sold in each machine.

PROOF OF CONCEPT

- **Revenue:** $700 per month in revenue from their best machines.
- **Distribution:** Locations secured in Halifax, including in a national branded hotel chain and a design school.

DRAGONS' DEAL

- **The Ask:** $150,000 for 25% equity.
- **Company Valuation:** $600,000.
- **The Deal:** $0.

START-UP ESSENTIALS: How to Conduct a Feasibility Study

You need to conduct a feasibility study to make sure that your business concept is worth pursuing.

1. TEAM AND ADVISERS

- Describe the background of the members of your team who have domain expertise in your product or service category and deep market experience in winning customers in your target market segment.
- Describe the access you have to the functional expertise that will be needed to round out your team.

2. BUSINESS MODEL

- Describe how you plan to make money.

3. MARKET FEASIBILITY

- Describe the size of your market opportunity.
- Describe the market you plan to target.
- Describe your competitive advantage.

4. TECHNICAL FEASIBILITY

- Describe the status of your product or service prototype.
- Describe the resources that you have in place to scale your business idea (i.e., produce volume).
- Describe the results of any product or service pilot testing that you have completed.

5. FINANCIAL FEASIBILITY

- Quantify your start-up capital requirements.
- Quantify your projected revenues in years one, two, and three.
- Quantify your cost of goods sold.
- Quantify your annual operating expenses.
- Quantify your annual profit.
- Quantify your projected break-even point in years or months.
- Quantify and qualify the source of capital to which you have access to fund your start-up.

6. CONCLUSION

Can you succeed with your business idea? This must be a brutally honest assessment.

In the opening section of this book, you've taken your business idea through a feasibility study. Now it's time to hone your business model. In the next section, we'll discuss the most critical component of a sustainable business—business model mechanics.

CHAPTER 4

AN INTRODUCTION TO BUSINESS MODEL MECHANICS

"The core of any business model is a great product."

—Dragon to Pitcher

> **BUSINESS MODEL MECHANICS**
>
> Describe how you plan to make money. Identify what you plan to sell, what you plan to charge, who will pay you for it, and where your product or service fits in the value chain of your industry.

If you have ever watched *Dragons' Den,* you know that the pitchers often realize within minutes that they are no longer inventors sitting on the pedestal that their friends and families may have put them on. They are the *chief revenue officers* of their businesses, and they are at the biggest board meeting of their lives. If they don't have a clear path to profitable revenue, they end up leaving the Den with no capital and, in some cases, a garage full of inventory that they will never sell. This is not unlike the world outside of the Dragons' Den, and, in fact, mirrors it. The difference is that the Dragons are nice enough to let the pitchers know in no uncertain terms if their idea has legs or if it belongs in the scrap heap.

However, oftentimes, pitchers with sound products or services are rejected in the Den, not because they don't have a winning idea, but because they fail to articulate how they will make money. That's where a **business model** comes in: a business model is *a way of making money.* This book gives you many different ways of making money with your product or service. If you read each of the following chapters with an open mind about how they could relate to your product, service, or invention, you might just find a revenue-earning model that fits your needs.

Keep in mind you could theoretically build any number of businesses around exactly the same product. That's because a product is the centre of a business model, but is not a business in and of itself— it can't succeed without a great business model. For example, imagine trying to get into the water filtration business. You might think it is so competitive that your business wouldn't stand a chance. But three visitors to *Dragons' Den* figured out different ways to make money doing essentially the same thing—water filtration. And each of the pitchers walked away with a deal because they were capable of creating and clearly articulating a way of making money that was completely unique.

BUSINESS MODEL COMPARISON: THREE WAYS TO MAKE MONEY IN WATER FILTRATION

	Q water *Season 5, Episode 9*	AquaOvo *Season 6, Episode 20*	Event Water Solutions *Season 6, Episode 1*
Revenue Model	Rents water filtration systems for a monthly fee to restaurants.	Sells water filtration systems for a one-time fee to individuals.	Rents water filtration systems for a per-event fee to event holders.
Product/Market Focus	Restaurant water filtration system and reusable bottles that can be sold to patrons.	Personal water filtration system and stylish cooler for homes and offices.	Event water filtration system and refill station for special events.
Value Proposition	Restaurants can sell filtered tap water to their patrons in stylish Q water decanters.	Individuals can drink filtered tap water out of a stylish AquaOvo water cooler.	Event holders can offer filtered water as a free service to attendees, and eliminate the need for plastic water bottles
Deal Terms	**The Ask:** $250,000 for 33% equity. **The Deal:** $250,0000 for 50% equity.	**The Ask:** $400,000 for 22% equity. **The Deal:** $400,000 for 35% equity plus 3% royalty.	**The Ask:** $100,000 for 20% equity. **The Deal:** $100,000 for 20% equity.

THE WARM-UP: BUSINESS MODEL DEFINED

A **business model** is *a sustainable money-making system* that describes the product or service you sell, the customers you serve, and your repeat revenue model. The purpose of a business model is to sustain your business over the long term, not just to provide a series of unpredictable, non-repeatable product sales. Every business model should contain three core components:

- **Revenue Model:** How does the business work and how will you make money?
- **Product/Market Focus:** What is your product offering and its most valuable features, and who is the ideal customer?
- **Value Proposition:** What are the reasons paying customers value your product or service?

Revenue Model: How to Make Money

It's no longer just what you make that matters—it's also how you charge that distinguishes your business from every other business in your product or service category. And as the chief revenue officer of your business, your job is to monitor and manage your business's revenue model. The revenue model component of your business model should include:

- **Revenue Sources:** What your business does that makes money.
- **Revenue Model:** How your business charges for what it does.
- **Scalability:** How your business is structured to handle sudden increases in customer volume.
- **Cash-Flow Timing:** When you get paid and by whom.

Product/Market Focus: What Sells

The product/market focus component of your business model describes the product features mix that customers will be most willing to pay for, and the description of your highest value customer. To define your product/market focus, describe your:

- **Product Offering:** The product description and the two or three product or service features that will provide the most value to your customers.
- **Target Market:** The demographic, geographic, and psychographic characteristics that describe your highest value customer.

Value Proposition: Why It Works

The value proposition component of your business model refers to the reasons customers will flock to your solution. To define your value proposition, start with the features of your business that customers will find to be valuable, and then determine what each of them means to the customer.

- **Problem/Solution Description:** What problem does your product or service solve and how does it work? *Example: Our immune-system-boosting teas ward off colds.*
- **Technical Benefits:** Why is your product or service useful? What functions does it perform? *Example: Our tea products boost your immune system to help prevent colds.*
- **Emotional Benefits:** How does your product or service make your customers feel better? What social values does it appeal to? *Example: We use fair trade suppliers and eco-friendly raw materials to reduce the carbon footprint of our supply chain.*
- **Monetary Benefits:** What cost savings will customers attain if they purchase from you? *Example: Our product takes half as long to make as our leading competitors' products.*
- **Proof Points:** How can you prove that your product or service works? *Example: In side-by-side tests, our product is chosen two to one over competitors' offerings.*

DRAGON LORE

"The core of any business model is a great product." And a great product can't succeed without a business model.

Another business that might seem too competitive to enter is the tea business. However, when three different tea entrepreneurs visited the Dragons' Den, they each came with a different plan to disrupt the industry. They had all previously generated revenue. They had a viable plan for making money. And because they were able to articulate their business models to the Dragons, all three pitchers walked away from the Den with a deal in hand.

BUSINESS MODEL COMPARISON: THREE WAYS TO MAKE MONEY IN THE TEA INDUSTRY

	Steeped Tea *Season 7, Episode 1*	Domo Tea *Season 5, Episode 5*	Atomic Tea *Season 2, Episode 3*
Revenue Model	Sells loose leaf tea and tea products through in-home party plans.	Sells instant organic tea powders through retailers and its website.	Franchises turnkey quick-serve tea shops.
Product/Market Focus	Loose leaf tea sold to in-home tea party attendees.	Authentic organic tea powders sold by direct mail and retail foot traffic.	Prepared hot and cold tea drinks infused with exotic juices sold to retail foot traffic.
Value Proposition	Steeped Tea's loose leaf tea tastes better than tea brewed with tea bags.	Domo Tea is immune system boosting, and because it comes in instant powder form, it can be made quickly if you feel a cold coming on.	The Atomic Tea specialty shop model as the Starbucks of tea.
Deal Terms	**The Ask:** $250,000 for 20% equity. **The Deal:** $250,000 for 20% equity.	**The Ask:** $50,000 for 20% equity. **The Deal:** $50,000 for 50% equity.	**The Ask:** $120,000 for 20% equity. **The Deal:** $120,000 for 50.1% equity.

START-UP ESSENTIALS: Business Model Mechanics

1. **Prototype** your concept into a functional and monetizable product or service. Some entrepreneurs end up producing hundreds of prototypes before they are ready. You just need one that works and that people are willing to pay you for. This is the **pre-revenue stage.**

2. **Beta test** your product or service to a limited number of people who take your product or service for a test drive for free, so that you can elicit feedback on features, potential pricing, and marketing ideas. Gather testimonials and references from partners and customers who enjoy your product or service beta. This is still the pre-revenue stage.

3. **Pilot test** your product or service to your first paying customers using a controlled launch to a limited number of real paying friends, family, co-workers, and colleagues who would be consumers of your product or service if they didn't know you. Gather more feedback and potential revisions for your product or service. This is the **"first customers" stage.**

4. **Soft launch** your product or service to a limited number of customers outside of your immediate circle of contacts using social media marketing to friends of friends. Create buzz through free PR and then tweak your product or service offering based on feedback. This is part of the **revenue stage**.

5. **Hard launch** your product or service to a broader paying audience through online marketing, search engine optimization, social media marketing, and whatever marketing methods are the most cost effective for your budget. This is also part of the revenue stage.

A business model doesn't exist without a product that a customer is willing to pay for. At the same time, a product is not a business in and of itself. That's why it's important to incorporate the basic mechanics of a business model into your product or service idea. But first, in the next chapter, we need to discuss how to determine whether your business should remain a hobby or whether it should be pursued as a viable business opportunity.

CHAPTER 5

ASSESSING YOUR BUSINESS IDEA

"You should not have spent the money you spent before you found out whether or not it was actually something that people would truly buy."

—Dragon to Pitcher

ASSESSING YOUR BUSINESS IDEA

Business ideas come from many sources including personal hobbies, inventions, existing businesses, and sudden inspirations. Determine whether you have a business opportunity that is worth pursuing. Then figure out whether you want to be a product developer or a person who builds a business around products and services.

Every week a seemingly endless stream of pitchers visit the Dragons' Den with a dilemma. Do they have a **business opportunity** that is worth pursuing? And if they do, should they stick to being a **product developer** and try to partner with other businesses that can help them commercialize their ideas? Or should they try to become a **business owner** and build an organization around their product?

Developing a product (or service) and running a business are two separate animals. Getting sidetracked trying to do both can lead to a journey that the pitcher may or may not have the requisite skill set for or the desire to go on. People who have the skill sets to come up with unique product or service ideas don't necessarily have the acumen to build businesses. People who have the skill sets to run businesses don't necessarily have the creativity to build winning products or services.

So how do you make money on a product or service idea if you don't build a business to market and distribute it? Or how do you make money if you are a businessperson but you don't know how to develop products or services? That's where business models come in. If you want to be a product developer, not a business owner, then you can license your product or service idea to another entity that has the infrastructure in place to commercialize your idea (see Chapter 6). If you want to build a business, not be a product developer, then you can use any number of business models to get a business off the ground. Or you can be a combination of both. It's a decision you have to make yourself, based on your interests and abilities, or it will be made for you by the dynamics of a ruthless marketplace.

Two entrepreneurial product developers who visited the Dragons' Den knew how ruthless the marketplace can be. So they came to the Den to seek financing and strategic advice. They came up with an idea for a product—a duffle bag that comes with a collapsible shelving system to organize your clothes. Their dilemma was typical of all entrepreneurs: Do they have a product or the basis for a business? And what should they do next?

RISE LUGGAGE[1]

Pitchers: Lee Renshaw and Sean Renshaw, Season 7, Episode 1

PRODUCT DESCRIPTION

A duffle bag that comes with an insert that organizes your clothes.

BACKGROUND

While travelling back and forth to see his girlfriend, Lee Renshaw became frustrated with how wrinkled his clothes became from sitting in a duffle bag. So he came up with an idea for a better duffle bag, learned how to sew a prototype, and visited the Dragons' Den to seek investor assistance to commercialize his idea.

PROBLEM STATEMENT

How to keep your clothes from getting wrinkled while carrying them in a duffle bag.

BUSINESS MODEL

Manufacture and sell the Rise Luggage bag, a duffle bag that organizes clothes using shelves that are sewn into the bags. The bag hangs in any closet.

PROOF OF CONCEPT

- **Protection:** Patent pending.
- **Revenue:** $7,000 in revenue to date and 100 units sold so far.

DRAGONS' DEAL

- **The Ask:** $100,000 for 40% equity.
- **Company Valuation:** $250,000.
- **The Deal:** $100,000 for 50% equity with two Dragons who bring an opportunity for licensing or to sell on television on The Shopping Channel.

THE WARM-UP: BUSINESS OPPORTUNITY DEFINED

A **business opportunity** is a chance to make money on a product, a service, or a technology. To evaluate whether your idea for a business should be pursued as a business opportunity, it's important to understand the difference between a product and a business.

- **The Product Developer:** Someone who develops a product who may or may not have the business capacity to commercialize it.
- **The Business Owner:** Someone who has a product or a service, or access to someone who does, and who knows how to build a team and an entity, execute a business model, and capitalize on products or services.
- **Assessing Your Business Opportunity:** Here is a series of hard questions to ask yourself honestly about whether your business should remain a hobby or be pursued as a business opportunity.

The Product Developer

The first step in assessing whether your idea should remain a hobby or be pursued as a business opportunity is to determine if you have the basis for a business or just a product. A product is not a business in and of itself because you don't need to set up a manufacturing plant, an office, and a billing department to commercialize a product. You can just find a partner to manufacture and distribute it for you. For a product to be a business, it has to have an entity surrounding it, complete with a steady stream of customers and a team to service them. If you determine that you have a good product, but not the basis for a business, then you should probably choose a licensing or partnership business model and plan to partner with someone else.

When two different honey entrepreneurs visited the Dragons' Den, they came as product developers of new honey products and as business owners of their own honey farms. But the honey ventures had two different products at the centres of their business models.

BUSINESS MODEL COMPARISON: TWO WAYS TO MAKE MONEY WITH A HONEY PRODUCT

	Honibe *Season 5, Episode 12*	Wendell Estate Honey *Season 7, Episode 12*
Revenue Model	Sells drop-form honey and powder directly to restaurants and online.	Sells premium pure honey through retailers and online.
Product/Market Focus	Dehydrated honey that comes in drop form and sprinkle form to add to drinks.	Premium creamed raw, all-natural, unpasteurized prairie honey sold in stylish jars.
Value Proposition	The product is dehydrated honey that comes in drop form and sprinkle form to make it easier to use and transport.	The product is a natural sweetener that is certified kosher and is extracted from the comb on a source-certified farm.
Deal Terms	**The Ask:** $1,000,000 for 20% equity. **The Deal:** $600,000 for 35% equity plus $400,000 line of credit.	**The Ask:** $200,000 for 25% equity. **The Deal:** $200,000 for 25% equity but with 50% voting control.

The Business Owner

If two entrepreneurs sell exactly the same product or perform exactly the same service, what distinguishes their concepts? It's the business model they use to commercialize their ideas. But before you choose a business model, it's important to know what type of business opportunity you may have come across. The three main business opportunity categories are:

- **Hobby Business:** A hobby business is a business that doesn't provide a meaningful amount of income. You can't quit your day job and survive on a hobby business, because it doesn't earn enough money yet. Typical hobby businesses are built around personal-service ideas or personal-use products. And the owners of these businesses often have no real intention to grow them into sustainable businesses or they don't know how.
- **Lifestyle Business:** A lifestyle business is a business that provides the owner with a salary and maybe a small profit. You can't expect to attract outside investors with a lifestyle business, because a lifestyle business typically only provides enough money to pay you a salary. You still might be able to sell it one day, but because there is no meaningful growth potential for your business, it's generally not a business that outside investors will be attracted to unless they can help you franchise it.
- **Growth Business:** A growth business is a business that is started to support a team, including the owner, and has the potential for significant growth. What makes it a growth business is that it has the potential to provide a meaningful salary to the owners, a substantial profit of 20% to 30% per year above the owner's salary, and the potential for high enough year-over-year growth that it becomes attractive to outside investors. This is the type of business that outside investors are attracted to.

When entrepreneurs show up in the Den, they come with products, hobby businesses, lifestyle businesses, and, in some cases, growth businesses. And some pitchers blur the line between being product developers, service providers, or entrepreneurs with real business opportunities ahead of them. One such business is a waste removal business. It's no secret that the waste removal business is a competitive marketplace. So when two entrepreneurs visited the Dragons' Den with their waste removal businesses aimed largely at homeowners undertaking renovations, they knew they had to come prepared with something unique. While at the heart of each of their businesses was a waste removal service, their plans for making money involved two completely different business models.

BUSINESS MODEL COMPARISON: TWO WAYS TO MAKE MONEY IN WASTE REMOVAL

	Rhino Bags Waste Removal* *Season 4, Episode 7 (Update)*	TidyTrailers.com *Season 3, Episode 4*
Revenue Model	Sells heavy-duty bags for $30 to $40 a unit to homeowners who fill the bags with waste. When full, the homeowner calls a 1-800 number and the company collects the bags for a fee.	Plans to franchise their business format across Canada. The company delivers trailers to homeowners and then picks them up when they are full. The company charges from 25% to 50% less than their competitors.
Product/Market Focus	Large heavy-duty bags and pickup service for removing waste from your home.	Discount trash removal trailers for removing waste from your home.
Value Proposition	Convenient innovative solution to waste removal and an alternative to metal dump bins.	Affordable alternative to other junk removal companies in the market.
Deal Terms	**The Ask:** $300,000 for 10% equity. **The Deal:** $500,000 for 50% equity. The company later got acquired by Waste Management Inc. without the Dragons.	**The Ask:** $150,000 for 30% equity. **The Deal:** $150,000 for 50% equity from the Dragon who brings the most franchise experience.

* Rhino Bags is now called Bagster.

DRAGON LORE

A product is not a business, unless you are able to build an entity around it that profitably supports the owners and the employees involved in the business.

Assessing Your Business Opportunity

Before an entrepreneur makes a long-term commitment to an idea for a product, a service, or a business opportunity, he or she should answer some hard questions.

NINE QUESTIONS TO ASK BEFORE YOU PURSUE A BUSINESS IDEA

1. **Does your product or service work** when you demonstrate it to people? If your product or service doesn't work, doesn't solve a real problem, and doesn't provide measurable benefits, then it's not the basis for a sustainable business.

2. **Are there similar products or services on the market?** It may seem counterintuitive, but if there is no other product or service like it, then this may be a warning sign that there may not be a market for your idea. Lack of competition is certainly not a disqualifier, but it is a warning sign.

3. **Will it take more than 90 days** to build your first prototype and get your first paying customers? Business ideas that take more than three months to get off the ground will take significant resources to keep alive because sooner or later your salary has to be paid. And there is also always a risk that markets will shift. So unless you are backed by investors who are willing to take the risk over the long term, this is a warning sign.

4. **Do the numbers add up?** Can you identify how many customers you will need to support your business? Do you know how you will reach them? Can you make enough profit to cover your salary in three of the next five years, based on an objective sales projection?

5. **Do you have social proof** that your idea will succeed? Have 100 prospective customers told you that they would pay you for your product or service if you had it on the market? Have you shown your idea to outside accounting, legal, or tax professionals to ask for their opinions on your idea?

6. **Do you have enough capital** set aside to start and fund your business and your salary for at least one year?

7. **Can you generate repeat revenue?** Products or services that people only buy once are not the basis for sustainable businesses.

8. **Would you be willing to pay for your product or service?** Would you buy your product or service for the price you are asking, if someone else tried to sell it to you? In other words, would you eat your own cooking?

9. **Does your idea pass the "smell test"?** Hoping an idea will work and knowing an idea will work are two different things. If you have financial, technical, and marketing questions about your business idea that you are unable to answer, these are warning signs that should not be ignored.

PART I SELF-STUDY WORKSHOP

A product or service is the basis for a business, but it is not a business in and of itself. In order to turn it into a business, you need a business model. In this workshop, start putting together the basics of your business model. Describe the background of your idea, how it will be used, and what general type of business you would like to operate.

BRAND STORY

1. How did your **business idea** come about?
2. What is **truly interesting** about your product or service?
3. What will your brand stand for in the future?

BRAND EXPERIENCE

1. What events **trigger the purchase** of your product or service?
2. In **what way** do you see your product being used or service being enjoyed?
3. In **what type of environment** will your product be used or service be enjoyed?
4. List every way in which a customer will **come in contact** with your business.
   - ❑ Brand name, logo, and advertising choices
   - ❑ Initial contact with customers
   - ❑ Packaging
   - ❑ Operational process
   - ❑ Payment process
   - ❑ Delivery process
   - ❑ Environment (i.e., where your product is used or service performed)
   - ❑ After-sales support (i.e., warranties, guarantees, support line offered)
   - ❑ Others
5. Describe the **core theme** that will be infused into every interaction with your customers.

BUSINESS MODEL OVERVIEW

1. Is your business model a **product** or a **service** model?
   - ❑ **Product Business Model:** Produce and sell a product.
   - ❑ **Service Business Model:** Perform a service.

2. Is your business model a **merchant** or **agency** model?

    ❑ **Merchant Business Model:** Sell your own products and services.

    ❑ **Agency Business Model:** Sell someone else's products and services.

3. Is your business model a **producer** or **licensor** model?

    ❑ **Producer Model:** Produce your own product or perform your own service.

    ❑ **Licensor Model:** License the intellectual property of your product to others for a licensing fee.

4. Is your business model a **franchising/licensing** model or an **independent owner/operator** model?

    ❑ **Independent Owner/Operator Model:** Operate your own business model.

    ❑ **Franchising/Licensing Model:** License your business model to others who pay you a royalty fee.

5. Is your business model a **traditional** or **game-changer** model?

    ❑ **Traditional Model:** Pick a pure business model.

    ❑ **Game-Changer Model:** Combine two or more traditional business models to disrupt your industry.

6. **Revenue Model:** How do you charge and who pays you?

7. **Business Model Statement:** Describe your sustainable money-making system in two or three sentences.

    ❑ Product sold/Service performed

    ❑ Customers served

    ❑ Repeat revenue model

8. Why is it a **sustainable**, long-term business model?

In this chapter, we discussed how to figure out if you have an idea worth pursuing or just a hobby business that you shouldn't quit your day job for. In the upcoming chapters we'll discuss a variety of business models, including traditional models like licensing, franchising, and retailing, and non-traditional models like crowdfunding, peer-to-peer sharing, and the subscription-box model. To get started, the next chapter discusses the licensing business model, which is a model for entrepreneurs who want to be product developers, not business owners.

PART II

LICENSING BUSINESS MODELS

Permit other individuals or organizations to license your product or franchise your business format.

CHAPTER 6

THE LICENSING BUSINESS MODEL

"What you have is innovation in an industry that hasn't had any for a long time. You just need to go knock on some doors and get the licensing agreement."

"Go to them and say, 'Okay, I'm going to license it for a 7% royalty, because everything else is taken out of the equation … all the inventory costs, all the marketing.'"

—Dragons to Pitcher

> ## LICENSING BUSINESS MODEL
>
> Develop a prototype. Achieve proof of concept. Establish IP protection. Build a list of potential licensees. Design a sell sheet. Negotiate a licensing agreement.

Without the **licensing business model,** many products or concepts may never have got off the ground, let alone competed in the marketplace. In 1888, Nikola Tesla's idea for alternating current (AC) electricity would not have been able to compete with Thomas Edison's direct current (DC) electricity standard without the distribution power of Westinghouse. The licensing agreement he agreed to with Westinghouse for his patents became the basis for a historically important battle with Edison over whose solution would power our homes for generations to come. Ultimately, Tesla's AC technology displaced Edison's standard and powers our homes today.

Ernő Rubik's famous cube would probably still be an unknown product called the "Magic Cube," had the idea not been licensed in 1980 to Ideal Toys, who launched it with the eponymous name we now know it as: the Rubik's Cube.[1] The licensing business model became the basis for the world's best-selling game product. And in 1982, Chris Haney and Scott Abbott's idea for a trivia board game called "Trivial Pursuit" would not likely have been able to compete in the board-game marketplace without the distribution power of Selchow and Righter and a licensing agreement. The licensing agreement they put in place became the basis for a business that displaced Monopoly as the world's best-selling board game.

Licensing works so well that even a major company like Starbucks chose licensing over franchising to augment their corporate-owned store model. Starbucks Licensed Stores penetrate high-traffic outlets such as bookstores, airports, and even grocery stores. Their licensing store model frees them from some of the regulatory hassles of franchising, while giving them control over core components of their brand experience. And they can still run their corporate-owned stores at the same time.

The fact is, licensing works and is being used by both inventors and established businesses to penetrate markets fast. So if you have a prototype invention ready, then you should ask yourself the kind of hard questions that the Dragons would likely ask you if you were to pitch to them: Is your product the basis for a business? Do you have the resources in place to turn your product into a business? Do you even want to run a business?

If not, then consider licensing your idea to a business or a third-party individual or entity that has the resources to commercialize it on your behalf. Marco Longley, a Season 7 visitor to the Dragons' Den, did ask himself these questions, and came to the Den with the clear goal of getting a deal with a Dragon who could secure him a licensing agreement. And one of the Dragons agreed—Longley was bought out of the product and received a perpetual royalty on all sales. And more than that, the Dragon so believed in Longley's ability as an inventor that he asked for a right of first refusal on Longley's future inventions.

THE HEFT

Pitcher: Marco Longley, Season 7, Episode 10

PRODUCT DESCRIPTION

An ergonomic snow shovel and rake attachment that helps you stay upright while working.

BACKGROUND

While cycling, Marco Longley from Richmond, B.C., was run over by a drunk driver, which resulted in severe injuries to his back. True inventors are inspired by problems that affect them personally, and Marco Longley is no exception. He went to work in his own personal idea lab to come up with a product that would help prevent further back injury. And he was looking to the Dragons to help him strike a licensing deal that will pay his family a royalty for years to come.

PROBLEM STATEMENT

How to keep your body anatomically upright while shovelling snow or raking the yard so that you can reduce back pain, fatigue, and the potential for serious injury.

BUSINESS MODEL

Marco wants to pursue the licensing business model with an agreement that will allow him to earn a royalty based on a percentage of sales. His product solves a pressing problem. It's a snow shovel attachment that can be used to make long shovels and rakes more ergonomic. The tool is a secondary handle that attaches in seconds to almost any long-shaft tool, with no moving parts or special tools required.

PROOF OF CONCEPT

- **Protection:** Has a patent pending on The Heft product.
- **Capacity:** Created five hand-carved, fully functional prototypes.

DRAGONS' DEAL

- **The Ask:** $25,000 for 10% equity.
- **Company Valuation:** $250,000.
- **The Deal:** $250,000 for the rights to the product plus a 5% perpetual royalty on future sales. The Dragon also required right of first refusal on all future inventions.

THE WARM-UP: LICENSING BUSINESS MODEL DEFINED

Licensing is the process of giving another entity permission to commercialize your product idea in exchange for a royalty, under agreed-upon terms and conditions. The reason licensing is so popular is because it enables inventors to commercialize their ideas faster and with fewer resources than they could on their own. To evaluate whether licensing is a good business model for you, you should consider:

- **Revenue Model:** You research and develop a prototype, achieve proof of concept, and establish your intellectual property rights. Then you permit a third party, called a "licensee," to commercialize, market, and distribute it for you in exchange for a 1% to 10% royalty (negotiable), a lump sum, or both.

- **Product/Market Focus:** The licensing business model works best for inventions that fill out the product lines of established companies that already have an established distribution network in place.
- **Value Proposition:** Inventors can get to market faster and with fewer resources than they would require on their own. Licensees spend their time screening inventions, then manufacturing and distributing proven concepts.

Revenue Model: How to Make Money

Inventors who choose the licensing route are in the business of researching and developing products that people need or want. To attract licensees, inventions should solve real problems, improve current products, or fill out the product lines of manufacturers who have already secured shelf space. This business model means you are allowing a third-party individual or entity to commercialize your product. In exchange, you receive a payment stream called a royalty, which may include an upfront payment. Because you have done all the research and development in advance, the licensee has the opportunity to go to market faster than they could on their own—and vice versa. So it can be a win-win deal for both you and your licensee. Ideally, you should maintain ownership of the intellectual property that you license, whether it be a patent, know-how, or even a copyright. The two tools you will need to understand before you try to license your product are the **sell sheet** and the **licensing agreement**.

The Sell Sheet

Once you have your intellectual property protection in place, you can start approaching potential licensees with something called a "sell sheet." A sell sheet is a one-page marketing piece that showcases your product in a way that creates interest in your potential licensees. Ideally, your potential licensee will sign a non-disclosure agreement (NDA) before you send them your sell sheet. An NDA discusses how the commercial value of your confidential and proprietary trade secrets will be protected. Be aware, however, that in many cases companies will just flat out refuse to sign an NDA because they don't want to restrict themselves. A sell sheet includes:

- **Problem:** What does your product do?
- **Solution:** How does your product work?

- **Target Market:** Who is the ideal customer?
- **Value Proposition:** How is it unique or how does it fill a void in the marketplace? How is it faster, cheaper, or more powerful?
- **Image:** What does it look like?
- **Contact Info:** What is the next step that the person reading the sell sheet should take?

The Licensing Agreement

While most business models involve many individual transactions with multiple customers, from the inventor's perspective, licensing may only involve one transaction: a licensing agreement between you and the licensee. That's why it's important to take the transaction very seriously by learning the language and the relevant issues to keep in mind when considering licensing as a business model to commercialize your invention. The process of negotiating agreement terms can involve discussions about exclusivity, time limits, minimum guarantees (or you shouldn't sign it), and royalty payments (based upon some industry standard against sales, profit, unit volume, or some other figure). Keep in mind this is just an overview, so speaking to a licensing lawyer in your product or technology category before signing a licensing agreement should be considered a mandatory step on your part. Here are some of the key licensing terms to understand:

- **Licensor:** The individual or entity that owns the property to be licensed.
- **Licensee:** The individual or entity that is agreeing to commercialize the licensed property.
- **Term:** How long the agreement lasts and under what terms the time frame may be extended.
- **Geographic Territory:** Where you allow the licensor to sell your product. You can restrict them to a country, a region, or even a locale.
- **Agreement:** The contract that sets out what is to be licensed and how it may be used.
- **Performance Standards:** Any minimum sales, payment guarantees, or other milestones that give you contingencies if the licensee doesn't, or isn't able to, accomplish everything they promise to do. Without a minimum guarantee, you are putting your invention in the hands of someone who may not be able to perform, so it is imperative that you have some sort of minimum guarantee.
- **Termination:** The conditions under which either party can terminate the licensing agreement, such as lack of sales, marketing, or other failure of performance.

- **Exclusivity:** Your negotiating position depends on the manufacturing, marketing, and distribution plan that the potential licensee has for your product. If the licensee is a small start-up with no previous history, then you probably won't want to relinquish that many rights. You'll also want regional restrictions because they probably won't be able to achieve your unit volume targets on their own. If you are dealing with a larger company, with a deep product line and a long history in your product category, then the terms of your licensing agreement might be much more favourable to the licensee.
- **Renewability:** Refers to whether the licensing agreement is renewable after the initial term, which may be three to five years.
- **Brand Use:** Refers to how you will allow your brand name to be used.
- **Quality:** Refers to how you will allow quality to be controlled.
- **Royalties:** What lump sum or percentage of sales, net sales (gross dollar amount less discounts or returns), profit, or unit volume is to be paid and how it will be tracked and audited by you, the licensor. This part of the agreement should also discuss any advance payment to be paid, and the frequency and timing of payments, such as quarterly or otherwise.

Product/Market Focus: What Sells

The opportunities for licensing your property are so diverse that it would be impossible to cover every type in this book. But keep in mind that the key differentiator for this type of business model is the property that is being licensed. And be creative in your thinking. You can license a product, a process, a brand, or even a machine. Here are some examples:

Licensing Type	Description
Product Licensing	Create a new product like a toy, a gadget, or a game, or extend the line of a product manufacturer that already has a distribution network in place for your category of product—like Rubik's Cube
Technology Licensing	License a manufacturing technology, a commercial design technology, or a software technology, such as a software program.
Format Licensing	Allow a third party to use your name or system for a fee. This model is different from franchising, where the franchisor has control over the employee training process. An example would be a Starbucks Licensed Store.

Value Proposition: Why It Works

Inventors who have the ability to research and develop valuable products or processes often lack the time, resources, and skills to manufacture, commercialize, and distribute their inventions. Licensing provides these inventors with a way to monetize their inventions, without the pressure and risk entailed in launching a full-scale business. The value proposition of this business model includes:

- **Royalties:** As an inventor, you can sign an agreement to receive 1% to 10% of the net wholesale value of your product. Your actual deal will depend on the norms of your industry and particular product category, as well as your negotiating position, so this percentage may vary considerably. In exchange for allowing someone else to capitalize on your idea and intellectual property (i.e., patent), you receive a royalty and avoid the costs involved in starting a business.
- **Time-to-Market:** It could take years to bring your product or service idea to market on your own. But if you sign a licensing deal, your product could be on the market in months or even weeks.
- **Comparative Advantage:** You invent the products and someone else commercializes them. People who are good at inventing products and processes might be wiser to spend their time inventing, and let an established manufacturer, with a distribution network in place, bring their inventions to market.
- **Distribution:** Companies that license products have the distribution networks in place that could be next to impossible for you to establish on your own. While keeping 100% of the profit on a product that you sell out of your garage might sound like a good business decision, it might be wiser to sign a deal that gets you a smaller percentage of a huge volume of sales.
- **Why It's Disruptive:** Licensing is not a disruptive business model. It's an established way for inventors to commercialize ideas, processes, and inventions.

DRAGON LORE

If you are more interested in inventing products than building businesses, as the Dragons always say, then licensing will get your invention to market faster and with fewer resources than if you set out on your own.

Serial inventors typically license inventions. But sometimes you can get such enormous press and buzz from an invention that you may decide to go it alone. When inventor Wayne Fromm visited Dragons' Den, he had a history of successfully licensing inventions and a brand new product called the Quik Pod that seemed to be a perfect fit for a licensing agreement. While one Dragon agreed that he should relinquish some rights for a 7% royalty, he had other ideas. He had a clear plan to go to market without licensing, and wanted the help of any Dragon who shared his vision.

QUIK POD

Pitchers: Wayne Fromm and Sage Fromm, Season 7, Episode 8

PRODUCT DESCRIPTION

An extendable hand-held tripod for taking pictures of yourself while on vacation.

BACKGROUND

Pitcher Wayne Fromm is a self-described serial inventor who invents for a living. To invent the Quik Pod, he produced 100 prototypes out of his home over many years before he came up with the final product. His hard work paid off as Oprah chose it for her O List and Jay Leno took it on *The Tonight Show*. This is not Wayne's first rodeo, as he is also the inventor of Disney's Beauty and the Beast Magic Talking Mirror and various Crayola and *Power Rangers* toys. He wants to use the funds and strategic advice from the Dragons to further market his new invention.

PROBLEM STATEMENT

How to take a self-portrait with a camera when you are on vacation without anyone else's assistance.

BUSINESS MODEL

Produces and sells the Quik Pod hand-held extendible tripod himself online, through retail camera stores, and on QVC. The product fits onto most cameras and smartphones. He has earned a gross profit of 47.9% per unit.

PROOF OF CONCEPT

- **Protection:** Quik Pod is patented and trademarked.
- **Revenue:** Sales in year one were $560,000 and gross profit in year one was $260,000.

- **Demand:** The product sold out on QVC every time the pitcher went on the show.
- **Publicity:** Oprah chose it for her O List and Jay Leno took it on *The Tonight Show.*

DRAGONS' DEAL

- **The Ask:** $100,000 for 30% equity.
- **Company Valuation:** $333,000.
- **The Deal:** $100,000 for 30% equity, plus online and marketing assistance from one Dragon who is looking to partner with the company over the long term.

START-UP ESSENTIALS: Licensing Business Model

1. Establish proof that your invention works by building a low-cost, minimal-time **prototype** that demonstrates technical proof of concept. Build a detailed list of use cases and potential consumers for your invention.
2. Understand the financial and market feasibility of your product by doing **deep market research** that includes an analysis of the competitive landscape, market size, and universe of potential licensees.
3. Speak with an IP lawyer to discuss **intellectual property protection** using either a pending or provisional patent on your idea before you submit your idea to potential licensees.
4. Make a **list of potential licensees,** including companies with product lines already on the shelf that may have gaps to fill.
5. Create a one-page summary, a **sell sheet,** that summarizes the key selling features of your invention and why the world needs it.
6. Establish a **licensing agreement** (or multiple agreements) that your attorney has approved, which includes deal terms and conditions that meet your minimum sales and payment guarantee requirements.

Licensing a product idea is a rapid market-entry strategy for getting your product out of your personal innovation lab and onto the market. But licensing an entire business model is a completely different animal. In the next chapter, we'll discuss franchising and how it can help you expand a proven local business format into other markets by leveraging the capital and personal commitment of other entrepreneurs.

CHAPTER 7

THE FRANCHISING BUSINESS MODEL

"I think you guys can make some money. I'm concerned about you two guys scaling this thing to be a big investment that we can get excited about."

—Dragon to Pitchers

FRANCHISING BUSINESS MODEL

Prove your business model. Document your operating procedures. Establish IP protection. Craft a franchising agreement with a lawyer. Meet all legal obligations. Start selling franchises.

After American Henry Ford and his team figured out how to produce a $500 Model T for the masses, he still needed a method for selling it. Selling direct was not a long-term option, because very few people lived close enough to Detroit to pick one up. Creating a corporate sales force was too expensive because the Ford Motor Company would have had to pay people across the country and manage them with neither the Internet nor cellphones to assist the company. The most viable option for Ford was to set up **franchise** dealerships—an ecosystem of independent businesses that held licenses to sell Ford's vehicles. Each dealer was an **independent business owner** who provided a sales outlet (i.e., a dealership) and service support, all following the proven methodology that Ford himself approved. Thus, the franchised dealership was born with Ford's company acting as the supplier of the product (i.e., the franchisor), and local entrepreneurs acting as the dealers of the product (i.e., the franchisees). This enabled Ford to establish "boots on the ground" in various regions of the United States.

Much has changed since the days of Henry Ford in the early 1900s, but the spirit behind the launch of a business is the same: Produce a viable product. Establish your first customers. Then execute your business plan on a larger scale using a business model that matches your resources and the goals you have for your business. Franchising is a growth-oriented strategy that can help you achieve your expansion goals, because it enables you to reach geographically diverse regions of the country without having to manage each individual business location. Independent owner-operators called "franchisees" put up the capital, run the daily operations, and work hard to execute your proven business format—all in exchange for ongoing fees that they pay you.

When *Dragons' Den* pitcher Nicole Hyatt first visited the Den with her Tan on the Run business in Season 4, she thought she had a proven business model that she wanted to expand across the country. She chose franchising as her business model because franchising would provide a way for other entrepreneurs to start tanning businesses. But getting the Dragons to see the light of day on Nicole's pitch proved to be more of a challenge than she expected: while they thought she had done well to promote her own business, they did not believe that her model was proprietary or leverageable, and thus was not investable, so she left without a deal. So she retooled, reduced her valuation slightly, and returned to the Den in Season 7 to take another shot at convincing the Dragons to fund her franchise business model.

TAN ON THE RUN

Pitcher: Nicole Hyatt, Season 7, Second Chance Show

PRODUCT DESCRIPTION

Mobile airbrush tanning salon.

BACKGROUND

The tanning industry is pivoting away from traditional tanning beds to the safer airbrush tanning process. Pitcher Nicole Hyatt is building a franchise system and provides franchisees with an operating model, equipment, and the training needed to make sure they apply the tanning product correctly to their tan-seeking customers. She came to the Dragons' Den to get funding to grow the business nationally in 100 cities.

PROBLEM STATEMENT

How to service clients who are too busy to travel to a tanning salon.

BUSINESS MODEL

Tan on the Run is a mobile airbrush tanning franchise. Franchisor Nicole Hyatt charges a fixed $200 to $400 a month to franchisees because she says that percentage-based franchise fees are hard for a franchisor to track in her industry. Franchisees turn around and charge $60 to $100 per tan and do up to 15 tans per day for clients in homes, offices, hotels, movie sets, and at bodybuilder competitions. The cost of services provided is $10 per tan for the spray product and gas to reach each customer. She would like to sell franchises in 100 cities.

PROOF OF CONCEPT

- **Growth:** Since she first visited the Dragons' Den in Season 4 her business has grown—revenues have grown from $50,000 a year to $120,000 a year, and the number of franchisees has grown from five to eight.

DRAGONS' DEAL

- **The Ask:** $50,000 for 30% equity.
- **Company Valuation:** $167,000.
- **The Deal:** $50,000 for 50% equity.

THE WARM-UP: FRANCHISING BUSINESS MODEL DEFINED

Franchising is an expansion model that involves allowing a third-party individual or entity to copy and use your entire business model. The reason franchising is so popular is because it allows an entrepreneur with a proven business model to reach new markets faster, and with fewer resources, than he would require if he did it on his own. The key issues to consider when evaluating whether to franchise your business to other franchisees are:

- **Revenue Model:** You perfect a business model, establish documented operating procedures, and develop a brand. Then you license your business model to franchisees who bring start-up capital, expertise, a local presence, and time to manage and execute your business model in their market according to your branding and standards.

- **Product/Market Focus:** Franchising works best for proven service concepts such as restaurants, retail outlets, moving companies, and businesses that depend on repeatable processes.
- **Value Proposition:** An entrepreneur seeking growth and new markets for a proven business model doesn't need to be physically present in new markets. Independent franchisees create the local presence and bring capital to the franchisor, in exchange for a license to use the franchisor's business model.

Revenue Model: How to Make Money

When a business owner has proven a business model in one location and wants to expand, they have a resource-based decision to make. They can build company-owned outlets that are self, revenue, bank, or investor financed. Or they can franchise or license outlets to other entrepreneurs who bring financing with them. And the decision is not always an either/or decision. For example, when the team behind Yankee Candle has expanded to new locations, it has used company-owned stores only. Yet when Tim Hortons and McDonald's have expanded to new locations, they have used a combination of franchises and corporate-owned outlets, and Starbucks has used a combination of corporate-owned stores and licensed outlets.

Here's how franchising works: One day you decide to expand to other locations, but you don't have enough capital or manpower to operate other locations. So you license your business model to other entrepreneurs instead by creating a franchise system. As the franchisor, you become the de facto manager of *other* business owners. Each business owner, called a franchisee, receives a turnkey business model from you, complete with a brand, a supply chain for products and supplies, advertising and marketing support, and a proven operating model that you have set up for them. In exchange, you receive a franchise fee (which can vary from tens of thousands to hundreds of thousands), marketing fund fees (such as 4% of franchisees' annual revenue), and an ongoing royalty (such as 3%). This is not a simple model to implement, and you will rack up serious legal fees paying a franchise lawyer to get started. But the spirit of franchising is that your franchisees receive a proven business format, operating manuals, training and support (site visits and full-time phone support), access to a supply chain, site selection guidance, and a regional or national branding campaign.

When screening franchisees, it's important to create a profile of the type of franchisee candidate you are looking for. For example, most franchisors have minimum net-worth and liquid-asset requirements. You could set standards that require that all franchisees have $300,000 in liquid assets and a minimum net worth of $600,000, for example. Also consider the personal commitment and business acumen of the franchisee to whom you are entrusting your brand. A franchisee who doesn't implement your operating procedures correctly could seriously damage your brand.

As you can see, franchising is a complex business model with many moving parts. So be sure to do research, attend a seminar, and seek legal advice before you commit to this model. Furthermore, understand the core concepts involved so that you can create a model that fits your needs:

- **Franchise Fees:** You charge fees that cover the cost of equipment, training, operating manuals, trademark use, and ongoing support. You can also charge a periodic royalty fee (e.g., weekly, monthly, annually), monthly rental fees if you own the buildings that the franchisees operate out of, and a monthly advertising fee (usually a percentage of revenue) to market the brand on behalf of all your franchisees.
- **Disclosure Documents:** Franchising is a highly regulated method of licensing and requires complete disclosure of your business practices through disclosure documents. Disclosure documents set out fees, rights, territorial agreements, franchisee obligations, minimum guarantees, franchise fees, and royalty fees.
- **Term of Agreement:** You can sign franchising agreements for set terms such as 10 or 20 years, or whatever period you determine. Your franchisees may demand and you may offer an option to renew the franchise agreement at the end of the term.
- **Territory:** Territories that you offer to franchisees can be exclusive or non-exclusive. Exclusive territories make your franchises more marketable and lucrative, but may limit your growth as a franchisor.
- **Financing:** The franchisee brings their own financing, but some franchisors provide financing support.
- **Operating Procedures:** While proving your business model, you'll need to document every step of every process that is required in product and service delivery.

- **Training and Support:** The costs of training and support are usually included in the franchising fee, but it's not uncommon to charge an additional fee.
- **Supply Chain:** You can either provide supplies to your franchisees yourself, or you can provide introductions and access to suppliers for them.

Keep in mind this is just an overview, so speaking to a franchising lawyer with experience in your franchise category is mandatory.

Product/Market Focus: What Sells

What inventions are to licensing, business formats are to franchising. You are coming up with a business model and are allowing others to commercialize it. The most successful franchisors focus heavily on perfecting operating procedures and building a proven, branded customer experience before they franchise. They build systems that can be replicated by other entrepreneurs who have little or no experience prior to being trained. To help you come up with your own franchise business model, consider the following format options:

Franchise Model	Description
Business Format Franchise	You provide both the product and the business format to the franchisee. The franchisee comes to you for a proven business model, product, and ongoing support. The franchisee then operates the business and sells the product.[1] Business types that work well for this model are services, like restaurants or rental services.
Product Format Franchise	You provide the product only to a franchisee, plus ongoing support and the right to use your logo. The franchisee runs their business and sells your product. Business types that work for this model include product-centred businesses like car dealerships, where little value is added to the product before it is sold.[2]

Value Proposition: Why It Works

Franchising is a business model that helps entrepreneurs to finance the growth of their proven business models. Instead of having to come up with bank loans or investor funding to open new locations, an entrepreneur with a proven business model can license his business model to a franchisee who puts up the capital to open up a new location. The value proposition of this business model includes:

- **Fees and Royalties:** You receive a stream of revenue from franchise fees, ongoing royalties, and, in some cases, rental income (if you own the properties that franchisees use to run your franchise).
- **Growth Capital:** Other entrepreneurs (franchisees) put up their capital to open new locations for your business concept. If you don't have the growth capital to open multiple locations yourself, entrepreneurs who want to franchise will finance your growth for you.
- **Risk Management:** If you open up a chain of businesses that you finance through debt financing or your own capital, you are taking on the entire financial risk of your business yourself. Franchising allows you to transfer a large part of the financial risk of opening up new locations to franchisees.
- **Turnkey Business:** You provide a turnkey business solution to entrepreneurs who have access to investment capital or debt financing. Entrepreneurs who buy franchises generally don't have the time to research and prove their own product or service ideas. They come to you because you've done it for them.

DRAGON LORE

If you have a proven business model, but lack the capital to build a chain of company-owned stores or service outlets, then franchising provides an option for you to expand to other locations.

When you have a proven business concept and you want to penetrate other markets, you have to act fast before someone else copies your concept. Your options are to grow the business organically using profit, franchise your concept to entrepreneurs who bring capital and sweat equity, or seek investor capital from disciplined investors like the Dragons. When Lori MacKenzie entered the Den, all of the Dragons quickly warmed up to her concept. And the fact that she gave one Dragon a free trial of her massage therapy didn't hurt. With a valuation that was right on the money, and a business model that was proven, she ended up receiving competing offers from two Dragons right on the spot. But were the offers enough for her to accept?

MASSAGE ADDICT

Pitchers: Lori MacKenzie and Chris Harker, Season 6, Episode 13

PRODUCT DESCRIPTION

A membership-based massage therapy clinic franchise model.

BACKGROUND

After injuring her back, pitcher Lori MacKenzie became so frustrated with the high price of ongoing therapy that she decided to take matters into her own hands. So she went out and proved a massage therapy business model called Massage Addict and came to the Den looking for capital to continue to franchise her business format.

PROBLEM STATEMENT

If a massage therapist knows how often a customer will be coming, they should be able to afford to charge their customers less.

BUSINESS MODEL

The company franchises a subscription-based massage therapy business model. Franchisees receive a proven business model and everything they need to open a massage therapy clinic. The cost to build a clinic in a strip mall is $150,000 to $200,000. Franchises follow a proven model, which involves charging customers an introductory rate of $39 to get them in the door, plus a monthly $59 membership fee in exchange for a lower rate on monthly massages.

PROOF OF CONCEPT

- **Revenue:** The highest grossing franchisee brings in $1 million each year.
- **Distribution:** Four proven locations in Nova Scotia and two in Ontario.

DRAGONS' DEAL

- **The Ask:** $125,000 for 10% equity.
- **Company Valuation:** $1,250,000.
- **The Deal:** $125,000 for 20% equity.

START-UP ESSENTIALS: Franchising Business Model

1. Perfect your **business format.**

2. Create a standard **operating manual** that outlines, step by step, how to implement every aspect of your business.

3. Research other **franchise agreements** to determine what the competitive landscape looks like.

4. **Attend a seminar** through the Canadian Franchise Association or the International Franchise Association.

5. Create a profile for the **minimum financial** and **non-financial** (e.g., industry experience) requirements that franchisees will have to meet to qualify for a franchise.

6. Create a **franchise agreement.**

7. Create a **training program** and support manuals for your franchisees.

8. Create a franchise **business plan** that your franchisees will be able to customize and implement in their geographic regions.

9. Create a **franchise fact sheet** that includes your value proposition, product description, development strategy, fees, and next steps.

10. Seek legal advice from a **franchising lawyer** who can help you put together the required **franchise disclosure document.** Franchise regulations vary by province and state, so it is imperative to not venture into franchising without the guidance of an experienced franchise lawyer.

PART II SELF-STUDY WORKSHOP

If you want to go to market faster, consider licensing your product or service, franchising your business format, or partnering with other established businesses. A good place to start is to look for businesses that complement your business, product, or service. In this workshop, develop a list of businesses, products, or services that complement yours. Then brainstorm ways to partner with them through a licensing, franchising, or partnership relationship.

SOURCES OF GROWTH

1. **What** are you selling?
2. To **whom** are you selling?
3. What is your sales and marketing **approach?**
4. What events (e.g., holidays, deadlines, purchases) **trigger** the purchase of your product or service?
5. What other products and services **complement** your product or service?
6. What **organizations or associations** regularly communicate to your target customers?
7. List potential partners or outside businesses that can help you cross-market your product or service.
8. What **agreement** can you strike with these strategic partners to cross-market each other's services?
9. Do you know intermediaries who can **connect** you with these businesses and partners?
10. What's your **go-to-market strategy** (in one sentence)?

STRATEGIC RELATIONSHIPS

1. What types of businesses **sell** your product category? Try to name 10.
2. What types of businesses **complement** your product or service? Try to name 10.
3. What specific **manufacturers** build your type of product? Try to name 10.
4. In what **regions** of the province or country would your business model work well? If you find opportunities in other markets, you could potentially license your concept to another business or even franchise it.
5. What types of products could you **bundle** yours with? Try to name 10.
6. Review your answers to the above questions, and try to **set up a meeting** with one or more strategic partners who can help you reach your goals. Summarize the outcomes that you expect from each relationship.

In this chapter, we discussed the basics of franchising. The key to this business model is to spend your time perfecting your business format and operating manuals. Then seek legal advice to set up the legal side of your franchise. In the next section, we'll discuss business models where franchising is routine—retail business models.

Part III

Retail Business Models

Sell your products, merchandise, or services directly to consumers.

CHAPTER 8

THE CONSUMER DIRECT BUSINESS MODEL

"It's interesting enough for me to take a taste of the deal. I like it. I'm going to buy one. I'm going to use it. Whenever I use a [product], I don't mind investing in it."

—Dragon to Pitcher

CONSUMER DIRECT BUSINESS MODEL

Manufacture a product or provide a service. Build an e-commerce platform online or conduct live product demonstrations.

We may not always love our politicians, but we can certainly learn from their ability to sell themselves to their constituents. They are willing to go door to door and ask for our vote. They'll stand outside of train stations in the rain, shake our hands, and hand out fliers. They work with limited budgets and hard deadlines to make their efforts successful. They don't worry about not having any sales skills because they know their passion will take over when they get in front of people. They start with a raw message that evolves over time into a razor-sharp message. They use any free PR to get their message out. Nothing is beneath them when it comes to asking for our vote. And they are willing to switch to a new campaign strategy if they are not getting results.

In business, sometimes the best way to launch a business is to use a political-style grass-roots campaign, otherwise known as a **consumer direct business model.** Consumer direct means creating a product and then picking up the phone, going door to door, or selling directly to the consumer through an e-commerce platform online. It may mean holding demonstration parties in people's homes to sell your products, in hopes of one day launching a party plan company empire with a team of sales consultants who do the selling for you. Or selling a gadget you invented in your basement to family, friends, and co-workers in hopes of one day landing a spot on The Shopping Channel or a licensing deal with a major manufacturer. The consumer direct business model gives every entrepreneur the chance to get their business idea off the ground because all they have to do is find a customer.

The consumer direct model is one that lets you build businesses quickly. When Marcus and Cam Dahl entered the Den, all of the Dragons warmed up to their unique concept— and the fact that they brought puppies with them. And while their valuation was just high enough to deter most of the Dragons, the couple was able to *groom* one Dragon who agreed to fund their expansion plans.

JET PET RESORT

Pitchers: Marcus Dahl and Cam Dahl, Season 7, Episode 7

PRODUCT DESCRIPTION

A luxury airport pet resort.

BACKGROUND

After being pressured by his wife to open a luxury pet resort for 10 years, Marcus Dahl finally agreed. He and his wife opened Jet Pet Resort outside of Vancouver International Airport, and after a year and a half in business, they came to *Dragons' Den* to seek expansion funding to open up in Toronto or Seattle.[1]

PROBLEM STATEMENT

Where to leave your pets while on vacation, if you don't want to leave them at a kennel.

BUSINESS MODEL

A luxury airport pet resort where pets stay for an average cost of $45 per night. The resort stay for pets comes complete with a grooming salon, doggy lounge, and treadmills. By the Dahls' locating the resorts near airports, discerning pet owners can drop their pets off on the way to the airport.

PROOF OF CONCEPT

- **Revenue:** $352,000 in gross revenue in year one ($65,000 in net profit after salaries).
- **Growth:** $150,000 in projected profit in year two and $250,000 in projected profit in year three.

DRAGONS' DEAL

- **The Ask:** $200,000 for 20% equity.
- **Company Valuation:** $1 million.
- **The Deal:** $200,000 for 30% equity, plus 10% royalty until the investment is returned. The pitchers requested that their $75,000 salary per person be guaranteed, but were rejected on that point only.

THE WARM-UP: CONSUMER DIRECT BUSINESS MODEL DEFINED

A **consumer direct business model** refers to person-to-person transactions, with no wholesalers or retailers between you and your customer. The reason a consumer direct business model can be successful is because it allows you to bypass intermediaries who either want too much of your profit, or refuse to carry your product or represent your service. The key issues to consider when evaluating whether a consumer direct business model is right for you are:

- **Revenue Model:** You create a product or service, add a gross margin to the per-unit cost of goods that you sell, and then sell it online (for small-value products) or through one-on-one live sales demonstrations.
- **Product/Market Focus:** Products that are amenable to live demonstrations for groups of people and are based on problem/solution or before-and-after pitches.
- **Value Proposition:** For the entrepreneur, the model helps generate revenue that can be used to establish shelf space with retailers.

Revenue Model: How to Make Money

The consumer direct model involves bypassing all intermediaries and taking orders directly from the end-user or customer. Because you bypass intermediaries, your gross profit per unit sold is typically higher than what you would earn if you were selling through distributors or third-party retailers. However, what you gain in per-unit profit you usually lose in unit volume. So this is a good business model if you are trying to get your business off the ground with few, if any, resources. It may not, however, be a path to a long-term sustainable business because it is hard to scale. The consumer direct model involves a variety of different sales channels. Selecting which ones to use depends on the type of product sold, unit volume needs, and product characteristics. Here are some of the consumer direct models:

- **Sales Calls:** Contact individuals, businesses, distributors, and retailers who have a need for your product or service. This model works best for high-dollar, low-volume sales that require an in-person demonstration. Sales presentations are typically face to face, with orders being taken in person and shipped or delivered later.

- **Teleselling:** Use a phone list to contact people who have previously responded to a marketing piece. Engage in person-to-person selling by phone and take orders over the phone. This model works best for high-dollar, low-volume sales that require a sales discussion before the customer places an order.

- **Peddling:** Pick neighbourhoods or open events that match your target demographics and conduct short live product demonstrations face to face or out of the trunk of your car. This channel works best for products that benefit from an in-person demonstration or before-and-after sales discussions.

- **Direct Mail:** Rent, buy, or build a mailing list. Design, print, and mail out a direct-response marketing piece. Then convert incoming calls into paying customers.

- **E-Commerce:** Create an online platform to sell your products. Use a traditional online catalogue, online shopping cart, and a call centre (could be only one person) to sell your products. Or use a less traditional model such as a subscription box business model, flash sales business model, crowdfunding business model, or any other peer-to-peer business model that you will read about in this book. E-commerce is similar to traditional retail where you sell low-dollar, high-volume sales that don't require a verbal or in-person demonstration.

- **Home Party Plans:** Set up in-home product demonstrations by asking friends and associates to host them. Pitch to friends of friends and give the host a percentage of sales. This channel works best for demonstrable products like home products, kitchenware, or apparel that the customer typically purchases anyway, but is unable to find locally.

- **Business-to-Business (B2B):** Sell to other businesses by contacting their owners, managers, or purchasing managers directly by telephone. Request an in-person face-to-face meeting when possible. Have a pitch book in hand, complete with references, a live demo, and any press you have received.

Product/Market Focus: What Sells

Consumer direct business models, or their business-to-business equivalents, work best with products or solutions that can be demonstrated to solve a clear problem. They also work well with commodities that people don't need to touch and feel before they place an order online. The downside of this model is that new businesses don't benefit from the "halo" effect that is garnered when established retailers and wholesalers decide to carry your product. When you are selling directly to the consumer, your reputation is your own, so the trust-building process can take longer. Here are some characteristics that your product or service should have if you decide to go this route:

Consumer Direct Product Characteristics	Description
Problem/Solution Products	Products that can be sold by stating a problem and showing how your product solves it.
Unique Selling Proposition Products	Products that have never been seen before that solve a problem, improve life, or do something unique.
Live Demo Products	Products that lend themselves to live demonstrations can yield higher results than products that have a longer sales cycle.
Artisan or Specialty Products	Handcrafted or custom goods that customers know they can't get elsewhere.
B2C (Business-to-Consumer) or B2B	You can use a direct selling business model to sell products that solve problems or fill voids for consumers, or to sell solutions that help other businesses.

Value Proposition: Why It Works

Distribution networks can be hard to penetrate with a new product, so using a consumer direct model to establish a critical mass of customers is often an easier and more accessible way to gain market traction for a new product or service. The value proposition for this business model includes:

- **Per-Unit Profit:** Selling direct gives the entrepreneur a higher gross profit margin per unit than selling through intermediaries because there are no intermediaries to pay.
- **Market Traction:** Going direct to consumers saves entrepreneurs the time and money it can cost trying to get into established distribution and retail channels.
- **Less Warehousing:** Entrepreneurs who sell direct can establish relationships with drop shippers who warehouse and ship their products, leaving the entrepreneur to focus on product development and selling, instead of shipping logistics.
- **Location Agnostic:** For consumer direct businesses that sell online or by mail, operating costs can be driven down by locating in low-cost areas of the country. Location of a business is irrelevant to a consumer who is buying something from you online or by mail.
- **Home Delivery:** For consumer direct models that sell online or by mail, consumers are able to place orders without having to get in the car and travel to a retail outlet.

DRAGON LORE

A consumer direct business model works best for entrepreneurs who are having trouble trying to penetrate established distribution and retail channels.

One visitor to the Den, The Aussie X Sports Programs, uses the business-to-business (B2B) version of consumer direct to sell in-school sporting programs. The B2B version of the consumer direct business model is exactly what it says: you sell your product or service directly to another corporate entity. The direct nature of this business model means that The Aussie X doesn't need intermediaries to find schools to pay them—all they need is a phone to present their sales pitch to a decision maker, and a website to show their demo videos. And because of the simplicity of their business model, they have not only been able to generate hundreds of thousands of dollars in revenue, but were also able to secure a deal in the Den.

THE AUSSIE X SPORTS PROGRAMS

Pitchers: Emile Studham, Kaela Bree, and Mark Sheard, Season 6, Episode 8

PRODUCT DESCRIPTION

An in-school sporting program that teaches three Australian sports: Aussie rules "footie," netball, and cricket.

BACKGROUND

Australians Emile Studham, Kaela Bree, and Mark Sheard found a gap in in-school sporting programs. They produce an Aussie-themed in-school sporting program that provides a higher level of service to kids than the schools can provide themselves.

PROBLEM STATEMENT

How to help kids become more physically active in school.

BUSINESS MODEL

The Aussie X Sports Programs sells and runs 60- to 80-minute in-school sporting clinics for schools and consumers for $2,500. For $2,500, instructors take over gym classes, summer camps, and corporate training events to teach kids (and adults!) their Aussie-themed sporting program.

PROOF OF CONCEPT

- **Revenue:** $220,000 in 2010 and $400,000 in revenue projected for 2011 ($80,000 net profit).
- **Demand:** Over 75,000 students have been taught.

DRAGONS' DEAL

- **The Ask:** $150,000 for 20% equity.
- **Company Valuation:** $750,000.
- **The Deal:** $150,000 for 50% equity from one Dragon.

START-UP ESSENTIALS: Consumer Direct Business Model

1. Get a **toll-free number** so consumers don't see long-distance calls as a roadblock to doing business with you.

2. Speak to an accountant about any **sales tax** issues that may apply to the sale of your product or service. Possibly speak to a lawyer to review any of your warranties, guarantees, and returns policies that might have a long-term impact on your future business liabilities.

3. Establish a shipping process and relationships with **shippers,** such as Canada Post, UPS, or FedEx.

4. Develop a **sales presentation** using PowerPoint, an online two-minute explainer video, or a scripted phone pitch that you can modify on the fly.

5. Build a web presence or **e-commerce platform** with an online shopping cart so consumers can place orders easily.

6. Use **Google AdWords, SEO, and social media marketing** to drive traffic to your web presence.

7. Use **PR** and charity tie-ins to drive traffic to your web presence or to make your phone ring.

The consumer direct model is a model that works well for establishing your first customers, selling online through a website, or, in the B2B model, for selling to other businesses. In the next chapter, we'll discuss the traditional retail business model where you open a physical store in a high-traffic area.

Chapter 9

The Retail Business Model

"At the end of the day, this is a pure marketing play. It's the highest margin, but it's also the highest competitive category … I want to do something with him because I like it."

—Dragon to Pitcher

> **RETAIL BUSINESS MODEL**
>
> Choose a merchandise category and theme for your shop. Find a high-traffic location. Test your retail concept using a pop-up store prototype. Create a launch event.

Major **retailers** and local specialty shops are under attack by faster and leaner start-ups that are using pricing mechanisms like flash sales and deals of the day to undercut them. They are under attack by "showrooming" consumers who touch and feel their products in store, and then buy them later from a cheaper competitor online. They are also under attack from smartphone apps that let people scan one store's products and point their shoppers to retail and online locations nearby that have lower prices. But savvy companies are not just sitting idle waiting for the next start-up to put them out of business. They are implementing **omni-channel** strategies that are making purchases location agnostic. In fact, many established retailers are so concerned about the marketplace that they are setting up their own internal start-up innovation labs that look and act just like start-ups.

Nordstrom Innovation Lab uses one-week time-boxed experiments to help clothing retailer Nordstrom (soon to open in Canada) come up with omni-channel technology and in-store iPad apps to counter showrooming by customers. The result is a buying process that allows customers to buy products any time and any way they want to, with little or no pricing differential. Walmart Labs uses an internal start-up incubator and Walmart's huge financial resources to conceive ideas that can be implemented globally in its retail outlets and via smartphone apps. It has an annual Get on the Shelf contest for product inventors. And it has even spun off start-ups like The Goodies Company, an online subscription box service that sends you a product sampler box once a month. And Procter & Gamble has a start-up innovation lab called Futureworks to explore ways of getting consumers to consume more of its retail products. The results include two chains: Mr. Clean Car Wash (yes *that* Mr. Clean) and Tide Dry Cleaners.

These efforts by Nordstrom, Walmart, and Proctor & Gamble are called "omni-channel retailing" and represent the future of retail. Omni-channel retailing means you build multiple sales channels, and then employ consistent pricing, shipping, and merchandise availability across all sales channels. By seamlessly tying smartphone apps, websites, and bricks-and-mortar outlets together, shopping, shipping, and pricing become dead simple, consistent, and tightly integrated. For example, you can allow access to smartphone apps that push store-specific discounts when your customers are physically in the mall; or you can allow customers to order out-of-stock inventory while in the store from your other locations, and have it shipped to their home for free; or you can allow customers to order products online and pick them up in the store. The omni-channel strategy is so disruptive, yet logical, that even Microsoft now has bricks-and-mortar stores, and online pioneer Amazon is reported to be contemplating getting in on the game.

But before you start building a smartphone app and dive deep into an omni-channel retail strategy, you have to have a store concept that stands out. Because retail competition is so fierce, you can't just open up a retail outlet and expect success. You have to be creative and specialize in something that will appeal to a specific niche. One visitor to the Dragons' Den was so creative that he had figured out a way to retail marijuana—legally. But even the huge profit margins on marijuana, a license from the federal government, and a million-dollar contract from one of Canada's territories might not be enough for the Dragons to invest. The Dragons do have their limits and sometimes they "weed" out businesses that they don't want to be associated with!

CANADA'S MEDICINAL MARIJUANA STORE[1]

Pitcher: Ian Layfield, Season 4, Episode 4
PRODUCT DESCRIPTION

A legal medical marijuana store.

BACKGROUND

Ian Layfield is a former road builder who was run over by a grader while at work one day. His doctors put him on OxyContin to numb the pain in his leg. After having three drinks with his medication one Christmas, he almost died. Driven by this life-threatening experience, he looked into the legalities of opening a medicinal marijuana store to give patients needing pain relief an alternative to prescription drugs. After starting operations, he came to the Den seeking "seed" capital to grow his medical business.

PROBLEM STATEMENT

How to retail marijuana legally.

BUSINESS MODEL

The company has a federal license issued by Health Canada to grow, package, and retail medical marijuana out of a mail-order store in Victoria, British Columbia. It services only patients who are licensed by the federal government to receive the marijuana for medicinal purposes. The model includes a gross profit margin of $10 per gram of marijuana (or $300 per ounce).

PROOF OF CONCEPT

- **Distribution:** Secured a contract for $1.2 million with Nunavut.

DRAGONS' DEAL

- **The Ask:** $250,000 for 10% equity.
- **Company Valuation:** $2,500,000.
- **The Deal:** $0 with encouragement from one Dragon to press on with the unique model.

THE WARM-UP: RETAIL BUSINESS MODEL DEFINED

Retail is a method of sourcing, marking up, and selling high volumes of merchandise to individuals through a series of low-quantity transactions—all out of a physical location. The purpose of retail is to provide **same-day carry-out service** in high-foot-traffic shopping areas or neighbourhoods to customers who prefer to touch and feel merchandise before they buy it. To evaluate whether retail is a good business model for you, you should consider:

- **Revenue Model:** You source merchandise from factories, vendors, and wholesalers at wholesale and then lease a location from which to sell them. You then sell at a 50%

gross profit markup using a repeatable pricing model such as keystone pricing (double the cost of wholesale) or some other methodology. Every retail segment (e.g., gifts, office supplies) is different, but your retail price needs to cover your cost of goods sold and a portion of the selling, general, and administrative expenses you pay to run the store.

- **Product/Market Focus:** Retail works best for goods that people want to carry out of the store on the same day, such as food; or goods that people like to touch and feel, such as clothing; or goods that people want to see demonstrated, such as electronics.
- **Value Proposition:** As the business owner, you can capitalize on foot traffic, so you don't need to spend as much money on marketing or advertising as a home-based business would. The customer gets to touch and feel your merchandise, with the added benefit of same-day carry-out service.

Revenue Model: How to Make Money

A **retail outlet** is a showroom with a cash register. When you start a retail business, you are in the business of procuring specialized inventory and then generating the highest revenue per square foot. Potential customers who walk into retail stores don't expect it to be difficult to find, learn about, or pay for merchandise. The Internet has spoiled them, and if you don't bring the Web's underlying conveniences to the layout of a bricks-and-mortar retail store, you probably won't be in business that long.

Here's how it works: As a retail business owner, you have many roles. As a **retail buyer,** you are responsible for procuring inventory at the lowest possible wholesale cost. To source inventory, you can frequent category-specific trade shows, magazines, or industry associations, or talk to established buying groups you find online. It's important to get to know their minimum order requirements and buyback terms, and to always request samples from prospective suppliers before making any commitments. As a **merchandiser,** you are responsible for creating displays, setting prices, and creating a shopping experience that maximizes your sales per square foot. You can source the necessary retail fixtures from specialty store fixture wholesalers. As an **employer,** you are responsible for hiring and training retail staff on product knowledge, sales, and customer service. And as a **marketer,** you are responsible for holding a grand opening, establishing a pricing model, launching periodic sales promotions, and social networking with the consumers who frequent your store.

Four retail models for you to consider are:

- **Wholesale Model:** Buy wholesale merchandise from a distributor or manufacturer at wholesale prices, and then mark it up using a repeatable pricing model such as keystone pricing (i.e., double your wholesale cost and then modify the price up or down by a set percentage). The downside of a wholesale model is that you do take ownership of the inventory, so you'll have to finance it until you are able to sell it at retail.
- **Off-Price Model:** Buy merchandise at up to 50% off wholesale using a retailer buying method called "opportunistic buying." Purchase end-of-season, overstock, or pack-and-hold merchandise from brand or artisan manufacturers looking to liquidate their surplus inventory. Use the discount you are receiving off the wholesale price to sell at deep discounts to retail.
- **Factory Direct Model:** Open a store to sell your own product line and then mark up your products by a set percentage. This model is operationally complex because you have to produce products that sell and run a retail shop at the same time.
- **Consignment Model:** Source inventory without having to pay cash upfront by finding individuals who are looking to liquidate their household items or clothing. Success with this model depends on having a *large number* of individual sellers of pre-owned merchandise, who expect up to 50% commission on each item you sell on their behalf. Retailers can also carry items on consignment as a portion of their inventory mix. You end up having to manage many products from many different individual sellers, but you don't have to finance the inventory, because consignors will retain ownership of the merchandise until you sell it on their behalf.

Product/Market Focus: What Sells

If you're reading this book, you are probably not thinking of opening a department store, a category-killer big-box store like Staples, or a high-volume discount chain any time soon. You'll most likely open a specialty store that sells one category of product/service, which you have chosen because you have a deeper level of knowledge about that category than anyone you've ever met. And you are financially prepared for the calculated risk you are about to take.

The key differentiators for this type of business model are the merchandise being sold, the wholesale cost and source of the merchandise, and your location. To find a good location, study foot traffic patterns and the demographics of neighbourhoods near prospective locations. Request foot and auto traffic volumes and average sales per square metre from commercial property owners, such as malls. And give yourself adequate lead time of six to nine months, if possible, before signing a lease for your shop. Some themes that are viable for independent start-ups are:

Store Theme	Description
Specialty	Sell one category of merchandise, such as candles, jewellery, electronics, furniture, clothing, or artisan food products.
General Merchandise	Sell a variety of different merchandise categories in one location.
Food Products Store	Sell brand or artisan food products from a focused category such as organic, gluten free, or chocolate.

Value Proposition: Why It Works

Retail stores offer the consumer the opportunity to touch, feel, demo, take home, and sometimes return a product in person. In other words, they are supposed to be showrooms. You can't get that experience online. It's a business model that depends and capitalizes on the foot traffic that malls or shopping districts attract. In exchange for monthly rent, location improvements, and the cost of a marketing campaign to launch your store, you benefit from foot traffic and therefore don't have to spend as much money on advertising as would a business that lacks a storefront with foot traffic.

But independent retail is not exactly the turnkey operation it used to be. To compete today, you either have to sell inventory that people can't buy from any other local retailer, provide services that online retailers don't provide, or provide same-day delivery. And because of the online world, you have to make it as easy to buy from your store as it is to buy from an online retailer. The value proposition of this business model includes:

- **Specialization:** You can provide more specialized service, product knowledge, and category-specific inventory than any big-box retailer can. Come-and-go sales associates and limited category shelf space make it difficult for chains to beat a specialty format that is executed properly.

- **Foot Traffic:** If you are unsure how to generate traffic for your business, then retail provides a way to cut down on advertising costs.
- **Sales Per Unit Area:** Statistics on sales per square foot are readily available from industry associations, commercial property owners, or trade associations online.
- **Cash and Carry:** Customers get the benefit of touching and feeling products that they can carry out of the store the same day.
- **Why It's Disruptive:** Retail in its traditional bricks-and-mortar form is not disruptive. However, using omni-channel, automated retail, and pop-up retail models in staid product categories is disruptive.

DRAGON LORE

In retail, your number one objective is to generate the highest volume of sales per square foot of retail space by augmenting your in-store sales with over-the-phone, online, and smartphone order taking.

While an omni-channel retailing strategy is dominating the thought processes of most retail store owners and corporate executives, some retail entrepreneurs stick with the basics. And in the case of Modrobes clothing pitcher Steven Sal Debus from Season 4, it is for good reason. He once built his Modrobes brand up to $10 million in revenue per year, and then was forced to shut down because his business expanded too quickly. So he came to Dragons' Den at what one Dragon called "back at the beginning of the race" and presented his plan for a thorough re-launch of his Modrobes clothing line and a Modrobes retail outlet.

MODROBES

Pitcher: Steven Sal Debus, Season 4, Episode 2
PRODUCT DESCRIPTION
An eco-friendly clothing line made from recycled materials.

BACKGROUND

Pitcher Steven Sal Debus owns a retail brand and outlet that is built around the concept of ethical consumption. To originally launch his eco-friendly clothing brand, he followed a traditional path to entrepreneurial success. He started selling his clothing line directly to consumers anywhere he could, including out of the back of his vehicle. He then built up the clothing brand to $10 million in sales. But after spending years building a national brand, he was forced to shut down for a few years because of over-expansion and financial problems. Fortunately for us and the environment, he decided to visit *Dragons' Den* to find investor capital to re-launch his brand.

PROBLEM STATEMENT

How to manufacture and sell sustainable performance clothing without going bankrupt.

BUSINESS MODEL

The company produces and retails an eco-friendly line of performance clothing called Modrobes. The company planned to sell the clothing line through a Modrobes retail outlet on Queen Street in Toronto. While that location has since closed, a new combined retail outlet and office has opened on Dupont Street in the Junction neighbourhood, where the company focuses on wholesaling operations.

PROOF OF CONCEPT

- **Revenue:** Previously sold $10 million in Modrobes product in one year, prior to shutting down the first time.
- **Demand:** Re-launched the Modrobes brand online and sold out his first product in 10 seconds.
- **Capacity:** Has invested $1 million into the Modrobes brand.

DRAGONS' DEAL

- **The Ask:** $200,000 for 30% equity.
- **Company Valuation:** $666,666.
- **The Deal:** $200,000 for 25% equity with $100,000 coming in cash and $100,000 as an operating line.

START-UP ESSENTIALS: Retail Business Model

1. Create **a theme** for your store by selling a specific type of category of product (e.g., jewellery) or serving a specific customer type (e.g., mothers, teenagers, or some other group).

2. Find **multiple suppliers** of consignment, wholesale, or factory direct products through industry trade shows or magazines. Start well in advance of your store opening. Limit your merchandise to niche products that are difficult to find elsewhere.

3. Establish an easy-to-implement **pricing model** such as keystone pricing (i.e., double wholesale plus or minus a certain percentage).

4. Look for potentially lucrative, **high-foot-traffic areas** that fit your customer profile. Peak hours will be when people are not working or going to school.

5. Acquire **business insurance** and talk to retailers about average utilities.

6. Acquire all required **licenses and permits** for your product/service concept.

7. Test your **retail concept** first with a pop-up retail store (see Chapter 10)—before you sign a long-term lease.

8. Create an **omni-channel strategy** that allows the customer to shop by phone, online, or using a smartphone app seamlessly.

9. Get the word out through **social networks**, local press (most pop-ups are newsworthy), brand tie-ins, and signage. Then build a following on Facebook or Twitter by signing up anyone who enters your store.

In this chapter, we discussed how opening a traditional retail outlet is a high-risk venture that should not be undertaken lightly. In the next chapter, we'll discuss a business that is proving to be both a rapid market-entry strategy for testing a retail concept and a full-time business for many—the pop-up business model.

CHAPTER 10

THE POP-UP BUSINESS MODEL

"You are fighting the traditional way of thinking in business, so good for you for saying, 'You know what, I don't care what the other guys are going to do.' The only thing you have to do is go prove your model by selling more."

—Dragon to Pitcher

POP-UP BUSINESS MODEL

Identify your pop-up business idea. Find a high-traffic location and negotiate an agreement. Create a branded temporary layout for your store. Hold a launch event.

In an ideal world, the decision to launch a business would be nothing more than a math problem. A budding entrepreneur would make a list of quantifiable outcomes for the business venture (profit, ROI, or some other metric). Then she would assign a probability to each potential outcome. With these numbers the entrepreneur would then be able to calculate an expected value for that business and make a decision to launch, and the profits would start rolling in. But even the fathers of probability, including Dutch mathematician Christiaan Huygens, would agree that entrepreneurs who make investment decisions based on math calculations are likely headed for gamblers' ruin. You can't just enter a market and stay long enough to make your business idea work. That's because you never really know if something will sell until you put it in front of real paying customers. Until you do that, your business is purely hypothetical.

But what if you have a game-changing retail or restaurant concept that you want to open up for only short periods of time, to capitalize on sales that happen only at certain times of the year? How do you travel from market to market, without making a long-term financial commitment to a lease? One popular method is called a **pop-up store.** A pop-up store is a temporary business that has no permanent location. Not to be confused with food trucks, seasonal kiosks, or local craft shows, pop-up stores refer to actual enclosed stores. Property owners have empty space. Malls have vacant stores. Bakeries have downtime in the evenings. And restaurants have downtime during sittings they don't service. So, now, smart entrepreneurs are convincing these commercial property owners to let them use their spaces for short periods of time, sometimes hours. And in some parts of the world, entire pop-up malls are being created to service the retail industry.

One company that visited the Dragons' Den that should consider opening up a pop-up retail store is Ten Tree Apparel. The company sells items of clothing and then plants 10 trees for each item it sells. The pitchers' concept is so unique that retail foot traffic would be sure to visit their store—if it existed. When the entrepreneurs behind the concept visited the Dragons' Den, they were looking for funds and assistance with marketing their brand, and a pop-up concept might just kick-start their sales.

TEN TREE APPAREL

Pitchers: Kalen Emsley, David Luba, and Derrick Emsley, Season 7, Episode 3

PRODUCT DESCRIPTION

A socially and environmentally responsible apparel company that plants 10 trees for each clothing item sold.

BACKGROUND

While in school at the University of Hawaii, pitcher David Luba fell in love with the environment. So he got together with two friends, the Emsley brothers, who had experience in the tree-planting business. They decided to create a company that would give back to the environment, while still earning a profit.

PROBLEM STATEMENT

How to start a clothing line that supports people, planet, and profit.

BUSINESS MODEL

The company sells T-shirts, tank tops, hoodies, and hats and plants 10 trees for every item sold. The shirts sell for around $6 more than a comparable item, and the cost of trees planted per item sold is around $3. They source their clothing out of Oregon. The trees are sourced using the contacts that the Emsley brothers made when they owned a tree-planting business. They also source trees through a third-party entity called ReForest, for trees planted outside the country.

PROOF OF CONCEPT

- **Revenue:** $120,000 in the first three months of operations.
- **Growth:** Revenues are doubling every month.
- **Distribution:** Currently sold in 33 retail stores across Western Canada.

DRAGONS' DEAL

- **The Ask:** $100,000 for 20% of the company.
- **Company Valuation:** $500,000.
- **The Deal:** $100,000 for 20% equity from a socially conscious marketing expert and one Dragon who has been involved in the planting of 3 million trees.

THE WARM-UP: POP-UP BUSINESS MODEL DEFINED

A **pop-up business** is a retail store or a restaurant that has no permanent address. You open a store for a limited time only (sometimes hours, days, or weeks) and then shut it down. The reason pop-up businesses are so popular is because the business owner doesn't have to commit long term to any one location. The key issues to consider when evaluating whether a pop-up business model is right for you are:

- **Revenue Model:** You make money on merchandise markups (using keystone pricing or some other pricing model) if you sell products, or on admission fees if you hold events, such as art gallery events.
- **Product/Market Focus:** The model originated as a way to capture seasonal sales for prom dresses, Christmas merchandise, or end-of-season merchandise for sports teams.

But pop-ups are now also used by entrepreneurs for concept testing, promotional events, and channel support for well-known brands.

- **Value Proposition**: The business revolves around a themed, branded experience and a following, rather than a permanent location. It may be in one location for one weekend, and then in a completely different location for another weekend. Or it may only open up once a year for a holiday or a single season to capitalize on peak selling periods.

Revenue Model: How to Make Money

When you start a pop-up business you are in the business of achieving short-term project goals, such as the sale of holiday, seasonal, or end-of-season merchandise. Rent can range from free, if an empty downtown core is looking to revitalize itself (see Popuphood in Oakland) to a 50% to 300% markup on rent if you are only there for a few hours or days. You make money directly on markups on your merchandise or indirectly through traffic that is driven to an online presence, another permanent retail store, or even to a future store (if you use the pop-up to build a following). Success comes from building a branded customer experience and then signing up a following through your online social networks so they can find you at your next pop-up location. There are several models to consider:

- **Touring Concept Pop-Up:** Set up a pop-up model that changes locations on purpose to capitalize on lucrative markets in different geographic locations with varying peak selling periods. Chef Ludo Lefebvre travels around Los Angeles and opens up his restaurant in temporary unused space for days at a time.[1]
- **Seasonal Concept Pop-Up:** Set up a holiday store once a year to sell a product category that sells its highest volume during a specific time of the year. Prom dresses, end-of-season sports merchandise, and Christmas merchandise businesses use pop-ups in shopping malls.
- **Sampling Store Pop-Up:** Set up a pop-up to generate PR for a product or service in a high-traffic mall or town centre. The store should allow consumers to experience a corporate or artisan brand in person. Kellogg's has a Pop-Tart pop-up to drive sampling and provide brand experience for its wide array of Pop-Tart flavours.

- **Concept Testing Pop-Up:** Use a pop-up to test a retail concept before committing long term to a concept or a permanent location.
- **Showroom Pop-Up:** Use a pop-up to display goods sold in other outlets or demo goods to consumers. *Wired* magazine has opened pop-ups to showcase technologies that they write about in their magazines.

Product/Market Focus: What Sells

The pop-up concept attracts seasonal entrepreneurs, start-ups, and even brand-promoting corporations for channel support. Boxpark Shoreditch in London, England, is an entire mall of pop-up businesses that are housed in retrofitted shipping containers.[2] The Sundance Channel has a television show about a Los Angeles–based five-star chef who opens a restaurant called "Ludo Bites" in random locations for two or three days at a time. And, of course, shopping malls have Christmas shops, prom-dress shops, and end-of-season sports merchandise stores that open up for a month each year. Pop-up is so popular that corporate brands are now using it as a promotional concept. Harry and David uses seasonal pop-up retail outlets to augment their revenue from corporate outlets. Professional sports teams like the Washington Nationals use pop-ups to liquidate end-of-season shirts, hats, and tchotchkes in the suburbs. And Microsoft uses pop-up kiosks and temporary holiday stores in Canada and the United States to support the launch of its products, including Windows 8 and its iPad-style tablet called "Surface."

What started out as stands selling fireworks in parking lots has turned into sophisticated branded stores. We even have mobile pop-ups such as clothing shops that look like food trucks. For start-ups, the concept is also proving invaluable to test business ideas, temporarily, before a long-term lease is signed or other long-term commitment is made. For a few thousand dollars or less you can lease a location from a tenant-starved landlord for a week or two. Then you can open for business temporarily, and see how the market responds.

The key differentiator for this type of business model is the short-term nature of the project being achieved in the pop-up, such as sales for a business, a product launch for a start-up, or a promotional event for a major brand. To help you come up with your own pop-up business model, consider some of the more popular product/market themes:

Pop-Up Theme	Description
Retail Pop-Up	Sell merchandise that you buy on consignment, at wholesale, or off-price, or sell your own products. Pop-up retail can work for many types of merchandise, but it works particularly well for seasonal merchandise such as clothing and accessories or jewellery.
Restaurant Pop-Up	Create a temporary restaurant in an unused commercial environment or during the downtime of an established business. (If the business only serves breakfast and lunch, pay rent to use the space at dinner.)
Brand Pop-Up	Create a pop-up where consumers can touch, feel, and experience your product or product line. Build a list of followers on Facebook and Twitter so you can promote your brand to them in the future.
Event Pop-Up	Hold gallery events for art exhibitions. Charge admission, charge other artists for access to display items at your event, or just sell your own items during the event.

Value Proposition: Why It Works

The pop-up concept allows you to test a business concept before you lock into a location that you haven't had a chance to prove yet. Long-term retail leasing agreements are cost prohibitive (sometimes $10,000+ per month) for many entrepreneurs who run seasonal businesses or businesses that seek out customers. It's an efficient way to get in and out of a market in a short period time, so you don't rack up high monthly leasing fees for locations that only provide foot traffic at certain times of the year. The value proposition of this business model includes:

- **Uniqueness:** Pop-up stores stand out by default because they are temporary. You have the opportunity to open an unconventional retail outlet that customers aren't expecting.
- **Brand Experience:** If you make your store engaging, a pop-up business gives consumers the opportunity to touch, feel, and purchase products they otherwise might not have access to in their local environment.
- **Temporary Commitment:** You don't have to make a long-term commitment to an untested market or an untested retail concept. You can open the store and shut it down in hours, weeks, or months.
- **Channel Support:** A pop-up store can temporarily support an online store or another retail location.

- **Seasonal Revenue:** Pop-up retail gives you the opportunity to capitalize on seasonal sales for products or services that generate most of their revenue in a very short period of time each year.
- **Social Value:** If you open a pop-up business, you are monetizing someone else's empty space. That space might be an empty retail outlet, a bakery that allows you use of its facility at night when it's usually closed, or a restaurant that allows you to fill their empty space at night.
- **Why It's Disruptive:** Pop-up retail outlets draw attention to previously empty locations. Passersby become intrigued by the temporary look and feel of a pop-up location (especially if it's in a shipping container on a beach).

DRAGON LORE

The secret behind a pop-up business is that your business has the benefits of retail traffic, without the expense of a permanent location.

Another product that has the potential to work well in a pop-up store is called "Funk-Off." The product was pitched on *Dragons' Den* and helps eliminate body piercing odour. The team behind the product uses it themselves, and they know a lot about body piercing and the industry. They could consider pop-ups where they provide body piercing services and their body piercing deodorant for sale in a branded pop-up environment at places like malls or other events where people who pierce are likely to attend. It would be a brand experience to match any pop-up out there! Given that they secured a deal in the Den, they'd be sure to have some foot traffic.

FUNK-OFF

Pitchers: Dave Buckle and Trevor Fronchak, Season 7, Episode 1
PRODUCT DESCRIPTION

An all-natural body piercing deodorant that comes in a lip balm–style container.

BACKGROUND

Dave Buckle and Trevor Fronchak undertook market research and determined that there was no solution on the market to deal with the body odour that arises around body piercings. Natural waxes and plant fats, combined with essential oils, have been treating bacterial and fungal problems on the skin for centuries. The team currently sells body jewellery at three body jewellery stores. They also say that there are more body piercing and tattoo studios than there are Starbucks coffee shops.

PROBLEM STATEMENT

Body piercings can generate a rancid smell because your body sheds skin cells that get stuck in the piercing.

BUSINESS MODEL

Produce and market an all-natural, antibacterial, antimicrobial body piercing deodorant and sell it through body piercing and tattoo studios and trade shows. The product has a gross profit margin of 67% and comes in a container about the size of lip balm.

PROOF OF CONCEPT

- **Revenue:** $36,000 per month if 500 stores sell 99 units each.
- **Publicity:** Successfully completed a soft launch.

DRAGONS' DEAL

- **The Ask:** $50,000 for 10% equity plus 10% royalty on sales until the capital is recouped.
- **Company Valuation:** $500,000.
- **The Deal:** $50,000 convertible loan plus 15% perpetual royalty. The loan is convertible into 10% equity within two years.

START-UP ESSENTIALS: Pop-Up Business Model

1. Set a goal, such as seasonal sales, concept testing, an event, channel support, or showrooming to drive traffic to your own website.
2. Acquire all required **licenses and permits** for your product/service concept.
3. Look for **vacant locations** in potentially lucrative, high-foot-traffic areas that fit your customer profile. In some countries there are pop-up districts. Give yourself adequate

lead time of six to nine months *if possible*. Look for specialty leasing through real estate property companies or intermediaries like PopUpInsider.

4. Look for **ultra-short-term, gross lease agreements** with an option to go permanent in some cases, with no revocation. Terms may be from a few hours to a few days or months. Seek legal advice before signing anything.

5. Acquire **business insurance** and try to negotiate utilities included in any lease you sign.

6. Spend as little as possible on **improvements and fixtures** until you have a proven concept.

7. If you don't produce products yourself, source consignment or wholesale products well in advance of your pop-up opening. Limit your merchandise to **niche products** that are difficult to find elsewhere.

8. Establish an easy-to-implement pricing strategy such as **keystone pricing.**

9. Set up a **payment processing solution.** Consider using a mobile payment processor that doesn't require a merchant account to set up, such as Square Canada.

10. Develop an **employee training model** to hire and train full- or part-time staff as required.

11. **Get the word out** through social networks, local press (most pop-ups are newsworthy), brand tie-ins, and signage. Then build a following on Facebook and Twitter by signing up anyone who enters your pop-up so they can find you at your next location.

In this chapter, we discussed a business model that allows you to pop up in high-traffic areas and then shut down just as quickly. In the next chapter, we'll discuss another business model that lets you pop up and shutdown quickly. Except this time you're popping up in people's houses. It's called "the party-plan company" business model.

CHAPTER 11

THE PARTY-PLAN COMPANY BUSINESS MODEL

"I looked at opening up a Pampered Chef type model in Canada … Warren Buffett bought The Pampered Chef [party-plan company]. I love your business."

—Dragon to Pitcher

> **PARTY-PLAN COMPANY BUSINESS MODEL**
>
> Pick a niche product line. Source inventory from multiple vendors or manufacturers. Create a party-plan format that reflects your niche. Prove your concept by doing it yourself. Seek legal advice and start recruiting independent sales reps.

To be a game changer, you don't have to place high-cost ads, knock on more doors, or even invent something new. But you do have to be innovative in some area of your business. In many cases, you can simply change the way an already established product or service category is being sold. Often, the best way to innovate is to combine business or marketing models from the past and apply them to established product or service categories.

Trunk Club is an online service for men that puts people in contact with a personal stylist by phone or by email. Once that customer agrees on a personal style, the company then sends the customer a box trunk full of recommended clothes to wear. You keep the clothes you like and send back what you don't. The business model is centred on having an inventory warehouse and remote personal stylists. Stella & Dot has a party-plan business model that uses trunk shows borrowed from the fashion industry. Independent stylists set up in-home trunk shows and take orders right on the spot at homes of hosts who invite people to the party. And The Pampered Chef uses a Tupperware-style party-plan model where independent contractor sales reps set up cooking shows in homes to sell kitchen accessories and food products.

In each of these cases, there is nothing life-changing about the products they are selling—reasonable substitutes are available at local malls or online. But when the value that these companies add is *how* their products are sold, the businesses themselves become truly innovative. The business model being used is the differentiator for the business.

One company that visited the Dragons' Den that knows how to differentiate its product category using **party planning** is Steeped Tea. And the team from Steeped Tea had such a compelling party-plan company business model, as well as real results, that the Dragons were competing over the deal. The key to Steeped Tea's party-plan model is that the company has a product line that can be demonstrated live in a social environment. So they held a tea party in the Den and ended up getting three offers from three tea-loving Dragons.

STEEPED TEA

Pitchers: Hatem Jahshan and Tonia Jahshan, Season 7, Episode 1

PRODUCT DESCRIPTION

A loose leaf tea party-plan company.

BACKGROUND

Tonia Jahshan wanted to be able to stay home with her kids but still earn money. While on a vacation with her husband Hatem, she discovered a loose leaf tea called "Cream of Earl Grey" and became hooked on the product. So she started selling a complete line of loose leaf tea and tea accessories through 15 in-home party plans a month, until she proved her concept. Then she and her husband adopted the direct selling model called "party planning" as a way to extend her success in in-home tea parties. They are seeking investor capital from the Dragons to fund a market-entry strategy that will help them penetrate the much larger U.S. market.

PROBLEM STATEMENT

How to make people aware of how good loose leaf tea tastes compared to tea made with tea bags.

BUSINESS MODEL

Steeped Tea is an in-home party-plan company that has 500 independent loose leaf tea sales consultants who hold in-home tea parties to sell Steeped Tea products. Their consultants sell an average of $500 per tea party with 25% commission going to the tea party consultant. The company sells tea kits to independent tea party consultants for $250. Each kit includes loose leaf tea blends and tea-brewing accessories. The profit margin to the company is 10%.

PROOF OF CONCEPT

- **Revenue:** $1.3 million in revenue this year, and three tea party competitors in the United States are doing less in combined sales than Steeped Tea is doing alone.
- **Distribution:** 500 consultants have signed up to sell Steeped Tea.

DRAGONS' DEAL

- **The Ask:** $250,000 for 20% equity.
- **Company Valuation:** $1.25 million.
- **The Deal:** $250,000 for 20% equity from two Dragons who bring deep financial and franchising experience to the table.

THE WARM-UP: PARTY-PLAN COMPANY BUSINESS MODEL DEFINED

A **party-plan company** provides turnkey business opportunities to independent sales consultants. The reason party-plan companies are so popular is because the model allows entrepreneurs to penetrate new markets without having to hire or pay a full-time sales staff. The key issues to consider when evaluating whether a party-plan company business model is right for you are:

- **Revenue Model:** You establish a product line, an in-home party idea, and a legal agreement between you and your independent sales consultants.
- **Product/Market Focus:** The model works particularly well for household products that people are going to buy anyway.
- **Value Proposition:** For entrepreneurs, the party plan business model allows you to distribute your product through reps across the country, without having to set up a franchise or licensing model. Independent sales consultants are provided with an opportunity to start and run their own turnkey business based on the party-plan model.

Revenue Model: How to Make Money

If you start a party-plan company, you are in the business of distributing product through independent, commission-paid sales consultants who hold in-home parties to sell your products. Your gross profit is your margin above product cost and the sales commissions that you pay to your sales consultants.

Here's how it works: You source a product line at wholesale that you can private label under your own brand name. Items to consider include kitchen goods, tea, cosmetics, or artisan food products. The cost to procure your products has to allow for sufficiently high markups to cover your own gross profit goals and a buffer for commission to independent sales consultants. You then develop and prove an in-home party method to demonstrate the product line. The party can be a one- to three-hour cooking show, a fashion trunk show, a makeover party, or a tea party to demonstrate and sell products to groups of 10 people or more in people's homes. Include in your costs product samples to compensate the hosts. Create a demo starter kit that includes an initial base of inventory that could be sold at $100 to $250 or more. Source order-tracking software to manage independent contractor reps' sales and commission payouts. Then start recruiting independent sales reps and hold periodic sales meetings or conferences to keep your team of reps on track.

Out of all the business models in this book, this is the one that you must absolutely seek legal advice for. To launch your business, you'll need to decide whether or not you will establish a multi-level compensation agreement, where sales consultants get paid on products sold by any sales consultants that they recruit, or whether you'll start with a single level. Each independent sales consultant's primary work must be selling your product, not recruiting other sales reps. This is a complicated legal area, so have a lawyer review your starter kit and contract, or have them help you put it together. Compensating sales consultants to recruit other sales consultants ventures into a legal grey area, and cooling-off periods and anti-pyramid laws must be strictly adhered to. This is not legal advice, so speak with a lawyer who specializes in setting up business entities and direct selling companies. For further information, visit http://www.competitionbureau.gc.ca/eic/site/cb-bc.nsf/eng/home.

Product/Market Focus: What Sells

For many people on the outside looking in, the party-plan business model has a less than serious image. For people who have had little exposure to the business, the thought of holding Tupperware parties seems like a career choice that is less than ideal. But that image took a dramatic turn when Warren Buffett's company, Berkshire Hathaway, acquired The Pampered Chef. The kitchen products party-plan company had 67,000 "kitchen consultants" at the time of the acquisition back in 2002 by the world's greatest investor, and sold for several hundred million dollars.

The most successful party-plan company start-ups build independent sales teams around unique, high-quality products that need to be demonstrated, and whose brands aren't readily available through local retail outlets. The key differentiator for this type of business model is the type of party held. To help you come up with your own party-plan business model, consider some of the more popular party-plan business model types:

Party-Plan Company Theme	Description
Trunk Show	Companies like Stella & Dot have independent "stylists" who hold in-home fashion shows for apparel and accessories called "trunk shows." The company pays 25% to 30% commission on sales at parties held.
Tea Party	Companies like Steeped Tea have independent "tea consultants" who find hosts for in-home tea parties. Steeped Tea pays commissions of 25% of sales generated at each party held.
Cooking Show	Companies like The Pampered Chef have independent "kitchen consultants" who find hosts for in-home kitchen shows. The Pampered Chef party-plan company pays out 20% to 31% on sales at the cooking shows to consultants who sell through in-home demonstrations.
Scrapbooking Workshop	Companies like Creative Memories provide tools to help people do their own scrapbooking. The company pays commissions from 30% to 45% of products sold.
Candle Party	Companies like Scentsy have independent "sales consultants" who find hosts for their scent-testing parties. The company pays 30% on sales.
Tasting Party	Companies like Dove Chocolate (through Dove Chocolate Discoveries) and Lindt have independent "chocolatiers" who find hosts for in-home chocolate-tasting events. The companies pay up to 40% commission on each chocolatier's personal sales volume.
Makeover Party	Companies like Mary Kay have independent "beauty consultants" who find hosts for in-home beauty parties. The company pays its beauty consultants up to 50% commission if they sell at suggested retail prices.

Value Proposition: Why It Works

Launching a party-plan company to sell your product line means that you are establishing a team of independent sales consultants who work on commission. Because every sales consultant works on commission, you cut down on the investment or debt financing you would need to hire an in-house team to distribute your product across multiple markets. The value proposition of this business model includes:

- **High-Volume Sales:** You receive repeat revenue from each of your independent sales consultants, who collectively generate high-volume sales for your company.
- **Low-Cost Turnkey Business:** As the entrepreneur who starts the party-plan company, you are providing a turnkey business opportunity to stay-at-home parents or people looking to supplement their income. In some cases, independent sales consultants earn a full-time living.
- **Social Selling:** Party planning provides independent sales consultants with an opportunity to make money while socializing. It also provides a network of support for new sales consultants.
- **Growth Capital:** As the entrepreneur, you can grow multiple sales territories at once without having to pay a full-time sales force. Independent sales consultants work on commission so you only pay them if they generate sales of your product.
- **Market Reach:** You can reach markets you might otherwise never reach because independent sales consultants will sign up from all kinds of remote areas.
- **Why It's Disruptive:** This model can disrupt any product category if it hasn't been used yet in that industry.

DRAGON LORE

When you are trying to find a business opportunity, sometimes the best approach is to apply successful operating models from other industries to an already established product or service category.

Two entrepreneurs who visited the Dragons' Den wanted to leverage the power of party plans to sell their Burger Stomper kitchen gadget. But they knew their company couldn't be built around a single product. So they planned to pursue a distribution deal with a party-plan company that was already in business.

BURGER STOMPER

Pitchers: Konstantine Balkos and Nikolas Balkos, Season 7, Episode 7

PRODUCT DESCRIPTION

A burger patty press that helps you shape the perfect burger.

BACKGROUND

Two brothers from Toronto, Nikolas and Konstantine Balkos, were looking to take a bite out of the market for kitchen tools that help shape 2.3 billion burgers per year in the home. So they invented and patented the Burger Stomper and established production, warehousing, and distribution for the product. They are seeking funding from the Dragons to fund a direct response media commercial and partnerships with companies like The Pampered Chef. And the Dragons responded with a deal that was almost what they asked for.

PROBLEM STATEMENT

How to make a uniform burger patty in under five seconds so that the burger cooks evenly every time.

BUSINESS MODEL

Produce and sell a stainless steel burger press for $30 per unit online, through independent retailers, and through partnerships that may include party-plan companies like The Pampered Chef.

PROOF OF CONCEPT

- **Protection:** The Burger Stomper is patented.
- **Revenue:** On pace for $200,000 in revenue this year.
- **Distribution:** Has established shelf space with 30 independent retailers.

DEAL TERMS

- **The Ask:** $245,000 for 35% equity.
- **Company Valuation:** $700,000.
- **The Deal:** $245,000 for 40% of the company with a 12% royalty until the capital is returned, which then drops to a 2% royalty.

START-UP ESSENTIALS: Party-Plan Company Business Model

1. **Source your product** in small quantities until you settle on specific brands.
2. **Perfect your in-home selling model** by doing it yourself repeatedly and fine-tuning your model.
3. This type of business is loaded with compliance issues. Hire a **business lawyer** to structure your entity so that it complies with all applicable tax and direct selling laws before you start recruiting independent sales representatives. Misrepresentation of earnings, pyramid schemes, and other questionable practices can get entrepreneurs into serious legal trouble, so be sure to pay for a legal roadmap for your direct selling company.
4. Design a **compensation plan** that rewards your independent consultants with commission and bonuses, while still providing you with an adequate profit margin on each item sold.
5. Set up a **training program guide** with standards and protocols for independent consultants.
6. Source and **license software** to track sales and commissions owed.
7. Set up streamlined **shipping or drop shipping processes** so sales reps receive their products in a timely manner.

PART III SELF-STUDY WORKSHOP

Retail is the process of selling your product or service directly to the customer. At the heart of retail is your sales process. In this workshop, describe your products or services and why they are valuable, and then come up with a pitch for selling them.

PRODUCT DEFINITION

1. What are you **selling?**
2. How does it **work?**
3. How is it different from competitors' products or services that are currently being offered on the market?
4. What **features, attributes, and benefits** of your product, service, or business will customers be most willing to pay you for?
5. Does your product, technology, or service offer something **unique** to the market?
6. **Where will it be consumed** or performed, and how does that impact your design?

7. Who are the **stakeholders** in your business, and what are their overriding goals?
   - ❏ The decision maker
   - ❏ The shopper
   - ❏ The user
   - ❏ The investor(s)
   - ❏ The bank(s)
   - ❏ The supplier(s)
   - ❏ The regulator(s)

8. What are your plans for **line extensions,** improvements to your current offerings, or planned obsolescence of your current offerings?

9. Do you have **legal protection** in place for any of your features?

DEFINE YOUR VALUE PROPOSITION

1. Describe your **ideal customer** in general terms.

2. Identify your product or service **category.**

3. What does your product or service do?

4. Describe **how your product or service works**—in micro-steps. Imagine your product being used or service being performed in a sequence of micro-steps. For each step, describe it in the fewest number of words possible.

5. Label each step and post it on a **storyboard.** Put sticky notes on a whiteboard, each containing a word that represents the step.

6. What is **novel** about your approach? For each step in the process, try to isolate what's novel about it, if anything. Perhaps you have a four-pronged approach, a single-stage process, or a specific input or ingredient that provides unique value to the customer.

7. What **superior outcome does the customer get** from your solution over competing brands and alternative solutions?
   Remember, there are three buying motives to appeal to:
   - **Functional Value:** Describes why your product or service is useful. *Example: It cleans carpets better because it doesn't lose suction.*
   - **Emotional Value:** Describes how your product or service makes the customer feel. *Example: By using this product, I am saving energy, and that makes me feel good.*
   - **Monetary Value:** Describes how your product or service makes or saves the customer money. *Example: In the first year of use alone, you will realize cost savings of 5%.*

8. Format your value proposition into a **single declarative sentence.**
   - ❑ **Fill In the Blanks:** *For [specific buyer type], [name your product or service] is the only [product or service category] that [What does the customer get by using your product or service?].*
9. **Revise and refine.**

THE SALES PROCESS

Step 1: Your sales pitch

1. What **problem** does your product or service solve? What need does it fill?
2. What is your product or service and how does your product or service **uniquely solve that problem** or meet that need?
3. How much do you **charge?**
4. What **proof/demo/sample** do you currently have that proves that the customer should need or want your product or service?
5. How do you want the customer to **place his or her order** (over the phone, in person, by fax, or over the Web)?
6. Link each of the last four responses into a single **60-second pitch.**
7. Pick up the phone today and **test your pitch** on 10 people you know. Keep a list of who you spoke with and how they responded.

Step 2: Where is the **first contact** with a customer made?
   - ❑ Website
   - ❑ Phone-in
   - ❑ Face to face
   - ❑ A store
   - ❑ Other

Step 3: How is the first **question-and-answer interview** with a customer completed?
   - ❑ Online form
   - ❑ Person to person
   - ❑ Other
   - ❑ Prospective customers aren't interviewed

Step 4: How is a prospective customer **qualified** once they contact you?

Step 5: What can you do to **demonstrate** your product or service to a prospective customer?

Step 6: What types of **objections** might a prospective customer have about your product or service?

Step 7: What is **required** to process an order?
- ❏ Contract
- ❏ Order form
- ❏ Credit card
- ❏ Cash payment
- ❏ Other

In this chapter, we discussed a business model that can help you distribute a line of products through independent sales reps who work on commission. It's a direct selling model that can help you expand a proven business model to many locations without the complexity of franchising, or the low profit margins of retail. In the next section, we'll discuss business models that tap into the power of affinity groups—membership business models.

Part IV

Membership Business Models

Launch a member-only business model where members receive access to monthly subscriptions, shared information, or deep discounts.

Chapter 12

The Subscription Box Business Model

"There is no $30-a-month model. You are joining a market that is so competitive that grown men are weeping in it."

—Dragon to Pitcher

SUBSCRIPTION BOX BUSINESS MODEL

Choose a product theme for your subscription box. Build 6 to 12 different monthly prototype boxes with 6 to 12 themed product items in each. Contact brand partners to discuss potential *unpaid* product-placement deals. License or build a subscription box platform online. Launch your model and build a subscription base.

With increased competition in various product categories like health and wellness, artisan foods, and beauty and skin-care products, manufacturers are welcoming new ways to promote their brands. And now savvy entrepreneurs are capitalizing on this need to compete by offering product manufacturers a way to reach affinity groups with sample-size as well as full-size products. This model is called **subscription commerce** and it's really taking off. These are not fruit-of-the-month clubs or wine clubs that sell their products at retail. Instead, entrepreneurs are striking deep-discount deals with product manufacturers, then packaging them into monthly shoebox-like sample boxes and selling low-price monthly subscriptions to people who want them delivered to their homes.

One business that might be ripe for a subscription box business model after visiting the Dragons' Den is BeautyGram. The company currently ships out a hot-pink box filled with beauty and wellness products on demand, in response to orders. Deliveries are made in a hot-pink, branded Smart car. But the Dragons couldn't see a competitive edge for the company in a very competitive marketplace. Since the company already offers a choice of six different boxes, perhaps it should retool its business model to add a subscription box service, and return to the Den.

BEAUTYGRAM

Pitcher: Jennifer Ruparell, Season 7, Episode 3

PRODUCT DESCRIPTION

Beauty products delivered telegram-style in a stylish hot-pink box.

BACKGROUND

Jennifer Ruparell is a certified aesthetician from Calgary, Alberta. She launched her telegram-style gift box business out of her home in Calgary. Customers can pick from six different themed BeautyGrams and have them delivered to their spouses, friends, or colleagues.

PROBLEM STATEMENT

How to pamper your girlfriend or wife with a gift other than flowers or a cheesy gift basket.

BUSINESS MODEL

The company procures beauty and wellness products, packages them in a hot-pink box that retails for $30 to $200 depending on what's in the box, and then ships them on demand using branded Smart cars to make deliveries. Profit margins are 30% to 50% per BeautyGram box sold.

PROOF OF CONCEPT

- **Revenue:** $50,000 in sales last year.
- **Growth:** On target to do $150,000 this year.
- **Demand:** 80% of clients are repeat buyers.

DRAGONS' DEAL

- **The Ask:** $100,000 for 30% equity.
- **Company Valuation:** $333,333.
- **The Deal:** $0, but was given the option of contacting one of the Dragons later in the year if she can achieve further proof of concept.

THE WARM-UP: SUBSCRIPTION BOX BUSINESS MODEL DEFINED

A **subscription box company** is a business that procures sample- and full-size products based on a theme and then delivers them in a shoebox-like container to members for a low monthly subscription fee in the range of $10 to $30 a month. The reason to subscription box businesses are so popular is because brand-name and artisan manufacturers are willing to provide these products at low cost (sometimes free), since they see this as free product placement into new consumers' hands. Entrepreneurs are able to lock in repeat revenue from monthly subscription fees. And members get access to wonderful product samples at very low prices. The key issues to consider when evaluating whether a subscription box business model is right for you are:

- **Revenue Model:** You charge a monthly subscription fee of $10 to $30 a month or more in exchange for sending out a box containing 5 to 10 full- or sample-size products per month.
- **Product/Market Focus:** The model works particularly well for repeat-use products such as beauty or food, or from artisan and brand-name manufacturers looking to encourage regular purchases through free product placement in the boxes.
- **Value Proposition:** The customer gets to try full-size or sample-size products for a low monthly subscription fee before buying the products at full retail price.

Revenue Model: How to Make Money

When you start a subscription box business, you are in the business of curating, warehousing, and shipping deep-discount (say 10% to 20% off wholesale) sample-size and full-size products in a specific product category like coffee, health and wellness, or artisan foods. In exchange for sending out the box each month, you charge a recurring monthly subscription fee in the range of $10 to $30, plus shipping. Secondary revenues come from upselling subscribers on full-size versions of the products through an online store that you set up.

Here's how it works: The customer (i.e., the subscriber) creates an account through your website and fills out a form indicating their delivery-frequency preferences (one-time, monthly, or annual subscription). Each month, you select and package a small number of items that meet the theme of the month. You then ship the boxes full of clothes, vitamins, health foods, or whatever specialized product your business is focused on based on monthly subscriptions or on-demand gifts. You can even create a standard box for men each month and a standard box for women each month. Typically, subscribers have full control of the service, can cancel anytime, and can also set their accounts to auto renew.

To launch your business, you'll need a place to warehouse and package products from manufacturers looking for free product placement. Plus, you'll need to buy, build, or license an e-commerce platform that tracks and manages subscriptions and recurring payments. Options for building an online platform include white-label solutions, scripts, or an in-house development team that you hire. Costs to get the website up and running can range from nothing, if you are a programmer, to tens of thousands of dollars if you build your own platform. Lower-cost alternatives include companies like AheadWorks, which sell subscription and recurring payment extension modules that you can plug into e-commerce store platforms. Alternatively you can buy an all-in-one solution from a white-label provider, such as Memberly, for a small fee.

Product/Market Focus: What Sells

If you think this business model is nothing more than a novelty, think again. Birchbox, a beauty-themed and skin care–themed subscription box service that reportedly has over 100,000 subscribers, has attracted $11.9 million in investment capital.[1] Trunk Club, a curated subscription service for men's apparel, has attracted $11 million in investor capital and has over 120 employees. And even Walmart has entered the subscription box space with a spinoff called The Goodies Company, which sends out a monthly "Taster's Box" of artisan food products.

The most successful subscription box businesses focus on repeat-use products based on product themes such as health and wellness, beauty and skin care, pets, socially conscious products, or even crafts for kids. But simply providing a box full of random goodies based on a theme is not the point of the business and will lead to cancelled subscriptions after the novelty wears off. To succeed, you have to feed a passion that busy people don't want to have to shop for each month. To help you come up with your own subscription box business model, consider some of the more popular product/market themes:

Subscription Box Theme	Description
Product Sample Box	Companies like KLUTCHclub, Birchbox, Love With Food, and Healthy Surprise send carefully curated sample boxes of 5 to 10 items for a low monthly subscription fee (such as $8, $10, $20, or $33 per month). In some cases, if you like certain items, you can buy full-size products from the subscription box service provider's website. This could serve as a transition business model to help a purchasing model business get off the ground.
Curated Product Box	Companies hire stylists who customize recommendations for customers based on online and phone interviews. Then a "trunk" full of customized products is shipped to the customer. The model is being implemented by apparel companies like Trunk Club and CakeStyle, who provide an online showroom, as well as a personal stylist online and by email who helps the customer develop a personal style. The companies make money selling clothing at retail prices and send out boxes of goods for customers to try on.
Necessity Item Box	This model might be the most sustainable over the long term for single-product themes such as wine companies like Club W, or artisan coffee companies like Craft Coffee or MistoBox that send you coffee for $15 to $20 a month. There are even razor companies, like Dollar Shave Club, that send out low-cost razors each month. These companies sell products that consumers use daily, so subscribers are less likely to cancel the subscriptions.
Craft Kit Box	Companies curate educational crafts for adults and children and send them out monthly. For example, Whimseybox sends out craft boxes for adults, and BabbaCo sends out monthly boxes filled with educational kids' crafts.

Value Proposition: Why It Works

Subscription box business models are popular because they offer a low-cost way for members to experience a random variety of product category samples that appeal to their personal needs and interests. In exchange, the entrepreneur receives a recurring revenue stream and operates a streamlined operating model because each monthly box is the same and is shipped out at the same time. The value proposition of this business model includes:

- **Recurring Revenue:** Subscription business models provide repeat monthly revenue not only from subscribers but also from upselling of products that people want to sample again.
- **Low-Cost Inventory:** Many subscription business models benefit from manufacturers who provide samples for free or at a 10% or 20% discount off wholesale. Manufacturers receive the benefit of a low-cost distribution tool for their product samples.
- **Sampling:** Subscription boxes in many cases are really just sample boxes designed to convert subscribers into paying customers for products they like.
- **Product Value:** Subscribers to subscription box companies receive $30 to $50 worth of usable product samples for as low as $6 to $10 (plus shipping).
- **Data Collection:** Subscription boxes are reviewed by subscribers, so the companies whose sample products are included in these boxes have a chance to modify their offerings or marketing methods, based on feedback from your subscription business.
- **Novelty Factor:** Subscribers receive a random box each month, so there is a surprise element to each box.
- **Why It's Disruptive:** Instant feedback from subscribers can be used to help the participating product manufacturers (vendors who provide the product samples) learn what works and what doesn't with their products based on feedback provided online through subscription websites.

DRAGON LORE

The key to keeping subscribers from cancelling their subscriptions is to curate product categories that subscribers regularly consume, and vary your theme monthly to keep it fresh and interesting.

When the entrepreneurs behind Panty By Post visited the Dragons' Den, they had big dreams and a product that would "make the postman blush." The Dragons were interested in the product line but cautioned that just having a product and a website doesn't mean a successful business—the company needs to build a brand so that customers can find the website. With the business only in its early stages, and a sky-high valuation, the Dragons weren't interested. Though the company was unable to secure a deal, they are still in business today.

PANTY BY POST

Pitchers: Natalie Grunberg and Lori Sholzberg, Season 5, Episode 9

PRODUCT DESCRIPTION

An online subscription service that mails panties to your front door.

BACKGROUND

Natalie Grunberg came up with the idea for a panty-subscription model based on offerings that she found in Paris, France. She injected her love of France into her business model and plans to sell subscriptions to people all over the world.

PROBLEM STATEMENT

How to give a discrete gift to your significant other.

BUSINESS MODEL

A 12-month online subscription service ranging in fees from $155 to $240. The company mails out French, elegant, or sassy panties once a month. The business is positioned as a gift service, where consumers gift the service to their significant others.

PROOF OF CONCEPT

- **Revenue:** Made $25,000 in the first year of business.

DRAGONS' DEAL

- **The Ask:** $150,000 for 30% equity.
- **Company Valuation:** $500,000.
- **The Deal:** $0.

START-UP ESSENTIALS: Subscription Box Business Model

1. Establish a **product theme** for your subscription box business, such as artisan foods, health and wellness products, or beauty products. Brainstorm 6 to 12 monthly themes that are in line with your overall company theme.

2. Complete a real-world **competitive analysis** by ordering one-time subscription boxes from four or five of your competitors. Analyze their websites, offerings, delivery processes, and pricing models to glean ideas for your own model.

3. Build several **prototype boxes** and elicit feedback from core groups of people who fit your target market profile.

4. Contact prospective **brand partners** to research cost and delivery terms for potential products to include in your subscription box. Look for companies that offer free samples, off-price deals, and companies looking for marketing opportunities for their products.

5. After you have tested and proven a prototype subscription box model, **assess your business concept** and develop a **business plan** for your subscription box company. Outline your go-to-market strategy, business model, team, financial plan for the business, and how you plan to warehouse your products.

6. License a white-label solution or **build an online platform** to market and manage your monthly subscriptions and recurring payments from subscribers.

In this chapter, we discussed a model for generating repeat revenue on a monthly basis. The subscription box model helps companies distribute and sample their products, while enabling members to test out a variety of brand-name or artisan products that they might not have come in contact with previously. As the entrepreneur who launches the business, you receive recurring revenue monthly if you keep your subscribers happy. In the next chapter, we'll discuss another membership business model—the community business model.

CHAPTER 13

THE MEMBER COMMUNITY BUSINESS MODEL

"If all you're doing is acting as a match-making service, anybody can do that … how will [your community] ever get bigger?"

—Dragon to Pitcher

> **MEMBER COMMUNITY BUSINESS MODEL**
>
> Choose a common interest for your community. Find a business model that fits the community. Build an online community platform from scratch or use a white-label software solution. Build a critical mass of members using social media marketing.

An online community is a group of people who come together for a common purpose. Unlike a social network like Facebook, where people go for social discovery, successful online communities are **vendor-neutral** environments that members join to converse and collaborate on common interests, such as medical treatments, academic research, or independent music. For years, the business model for an online member community was advertising. But creative entrepreneurs have come up with more value-oriented models that enhance and further the interests of the member community as a whole.

Music communities like ReverbNation connect millions of independent artists, music industry professionals, and fans. Its business model is based on charging a monthly fee to musicians who want premium features such as digital distribution of their music through Amazon, iTunes, and Spotify. Peer-review communities like Academia.edu connect millions of academics with each other, so they can accelerate their academic research.

Its business model is based on charging third-party entities to access the research of its members. Learning communities like Italki connect hundreds of thousands of language students with language tutors from around the world using peer-to-peer interactions. Italki's business model is based on charging a 15% commission on any peer-to-peer tutoring that happens between the members of the community.

On the surface, these communities appear to be nothing more than shared-interest groups online. But when you dig below the surface, you find a variety of cutting-edge business models that make e-commerce and cost-per-click advertising models look like things of the past. They leverage the collective intelligence of the community members to solve real-world social, cultural, and scientific problems. None of these communities use e-commerce or social discovery as their primary way to attract millions of members. Nor do they use advertising as their sole source of revenue. Instead, they provide community-building tools that enhance peer-to-peer interactions and have a community-wide shared purpose.

As you can see, the core business of a community is not advertising. It's any transaction that takes place between the community members. If you try to build an online community and expect to generate substantial revenues from advertising, you'll need high-volume traffic that most start-ups are incapable of generating. Communities need creative business models to gain market traction. Unfortunately, the team behind AgriConnect brought an advertising business model to the Den and the Dragons had deep concerns about it.

AGRICONNECT

Pitchers: Frank Campbell and Jeff Schneider, Season 5, Episode 6

PRODUCT DESCRIPTION

An online community where farmers meet farmsitters.[1]

BACKGROUND

There are 229,000+ farms in Canada, and the team from AgriConnect wanted to capitalize on their need for farmsitters. So, they built an online community that has been up and running for 18 months. The company believes they can generate between $1.2 and $1.5 million in advertising revenue in the next three years.

PROBLEM STATEMENT

When farmers get sick or need to travel, they need farmsitters to look after their farms while they are away.

BUSINESS MODEL

The company makes money by selling targeted advertising to farm-related industries. The website is a community where farmers meet farmsitters.

PROOF OF CONCEPT

- **Funding:** Secured government grants in their first year of business.
- **Revenue:** $30,000+ in revenue in the last 12 months.
- **Demand:** Over 300 people, from Ontario to Alberta, are members of their website, and 169 people have requested the farmsitting service so far.
- **Traffic:** 800 to 1,200 new visitors to the website every month and 40,000 hits.

DRAGONS' DEAL

- **The Ask:** $72,000 for 40% equity.
- **Company Valuation:** $180,000.
- **The Deal:** $0.

THE WARM-UP: MEMBER COMMUNITY BUSINESS MODEL DEFINED

A **member community business** is an online platform where members share information on a common interest. The reason member communities are so popular is because they are vendor-neutral environments where the common interest of the members takes precedence over the commercial interests of the community organizer (i.e., the entrepreneur). The key issues to consider when evaluating whether a member community business model is right for you are:

- **Revenue Model:** Charge fees for tools that enhance or facilitate interactions between members, called peer-to-peer interactions.

- **Product/Market Focus:** Shared interest groups such as patients, academics, or entrepreneurs.
- **Value Proposition:** The value of a community to its members is the collective intelligence of a large group of people who share a common interest.

Revenue Model: How to Make Money

People join communities primarily to engage in constructive conversations and to share information—not to be sold products and services. If you don't understand that, then don't launch an online community. To make a community successful, it has to be hyper-focused around a group of people with a common interest. And it has to have a plan to be revenue-funded at some point in the future. The community business model can be big business if you are able to reach a critical mass of members. Two major community model successes are Care2, which has over 21 million members, brings together people with an interest in healthy and green living, and is revenue-funded by pay-per-action lead generation,[2] and ReverbNation, which has over 2 million music industry members, and is revenue-funded by digital distribution tools and contextual advertising.[3]

Here's how it works: As the community organizer, you build a community platform where members can create profiles. Profiles are webpages that describe the member's interests and any details he or she wants to share that relate to the core purpose and shared interests of the community. You can design and build your platform internally, use a white-label solution from a white-label provider like ONEsite, or use a pre-branded community-building application online like Hoop.la. To encourage interactions between members of your community, be sure to choose a platform that provides community-building tools such as blogs, social-network sharing tools, and forum or chat components. In exchange for building and maintaining the community, you can charge fees using any combination of the following revenue models:

- **Subscription Model:** Charge a monthly subscription fee to members for access to the community. For example, Angie's List charges members a monthly fee to access community-member reviews of home service companies. The subscription fee ranges from $1.50 per month up.

- **Pay-Per-Action Lead Model:** Provide contextual advertisers with access to your community through opt-in fee-per-lead forms. For example, Care2 charges non-profits a fee for leads generated when community members take certain actions, such as agreeing to fill out a form.
- **Recruiter Model:** Charge fees to third-party entities for job listings on a community job board. For example, Academia.edu lists jobs in fields that interest community members, such as science or higher education, in exchange for a $300 monthly fee.
- **Student-Tutor Model:** Provide community members with access to subject-matter experts and keep a commission on fees charged between members. For example, Italki charges a 15% commission to tutors who connect and interact live with students in the Italki community.
- **Data-Sharing Model:** With transparency, permission, and advanced disclosure to community members, sell scrubbed, non-personally-identifiable data to third-party commercial or non-profit entities looking to improve their R&D efforts. This model works best in the academic and health-care communities where members are seeking time-sensitive cures to survive or peer-reviews to improve their academic research.
- **E-Commerce Model:** Create a community store where you can sell community-related products or services to community members. For example, Gap Year charges members a fee for travel services for students looking to travel during a gap year.
- **Digital Distribution Model:** Create a community where artists or authors share samples of their work (e.g., music, videos, book summaries) and are given tools that facilitate the digital distribution of their work. Then charge a transaction fee.

Product/Market Focus: What Sells

Online communities are large, growing social interest groups that help distribute digital intellectual property, facilitate peer reviews, or help members engage in peer-to-peer interactions. There are many different community types to consider when building an online community. The most successful communities have a singular focus and put the common interest of the members first. Social discovery and commercialization take an incidental role in the community. And advertising is the business model of last resort. To help you come up with your own community business model, consider some of the more popular product/market themes:

Community Theme	Description
Social Cataloguing Communities	You create a free or paid, member-only community where members catalogue their product preferences so other members of the community can see them and buy them (e.g., Shelfari, aNnobii, Foursquare).
Peer-Review Communities	You create a free or paid, member-only community where people share their work and converse with their peers for feedback on their work to advance their work. To make money, you charge third parties to access anonymous data that can help them commercialize products or further their R&D (e.g., ResearchGate).
Vendor-Review Communities	You create a free or paid, member-only community where consumers share their opinions of vendors they use, and then charge a subscription fee to anyone who wants to access the trusted reviews (e.g., Angie's List).
Learning Communities	You create a free or paid, member-only community where members can interact and learn from each other through student-tutor, peer-to-peer interactions such as a language-learning community (e.g., Italki).
Patient Communities	You create a free, member-only community where patients share treatment history with other patients to advance medicine and improve the R&D efforts of pharmaceutical companies (e.g., PatientsLikeMe, DailyStrength).
Independent Artist Communities	You create a free, member-only community where independent artists can share their music or art, and then converse and collaborate with fans and industry professionals. To make money, you charge artists monthly subscription fees to access premium features that include getting their art distributed through iTunes, Amazon, or Spotify (e.g., ReverbNation, deviantART).

Value Proposition: Why It Works

Online communities are popular because they help individuals share information and further a common, community-wide topic of interest. They allow individuals to tap into the collective intelligence of a large group of people. And they provide a trusted, member-only environment that is monitored by you, the entrepreneur. The value proposition of this business model includes:

- **User-Generated Content:** User-generated content such as member profiles, uploaded documents, and ongoing conversations on a focused topic of interest keep the community fresh.

- **Collective Intelligence:** Members can help each other solve specific problems by sharing their own experience and knowledge with others.
- **Collaboration:** Members can share ideas and experience, get inspired, and find people to collaborate with to achieve a shared purpose.
- **Social Discovery:** The main purpose of an online community is information sharing, but meeting others is a natural side effect.
- **Fostered Learning:** A large group of people are sharing information on a single topic of interest, which its members can use to learn.
- **Crowdsourcing:** You can enact change when a large community builds user-generated content into a de facto knowledge base for solving problems in a single area of interest.
- **Why It's Disruptive:** Online membership communities are not disruptive. They have been around for over a decade.

DRAGON LORE

Try to find a white-label community-website solution that can be licensed at a lower cost than it would cost to build your own from scratch.

START-UP ESSENTIALS: Member Community Business Model

1. Create a community **mission statement** to state why your community will exist (e.g., determine what shared interest or shared purpose will be the theme of your community).
2. Describe **who will be your members** and make a list of conversation starters or dialogue themes.
3. Define any **user-generated content** (e.g., research papers uploaded, music uploads).
4. Determine what will be **monetized** in your community (e.g., job listings, shareable data, peer-to-peer tutoring or transactions).
5. Map out your **information-sharing tools** (e.g., profile pages, upload capabilities, profile view analytics, communication tools).
6. Define the **user-generated content** that will keep community members coming back again and again (e.g., blog posts, video uploads, information sharing).

7. Establish **community guidelines.**

8. Find/identify a **business model (or models)** for the community.

9. Create an **online platform** by programing it yourself, using a white-label platform from a provider like ONEsite, or by using a pop-up platform from an entry-level solution like Hoop.la or Socious.

10. **Soft launch** your community through social media marketing efforts to build a critical mass of members who interact with each other and provide feedback on your community and your community-building features.

11. **Hard launch** your community with SEO, a Google AdWords campaign, PR, social media sharing tools, and ongoing social media marketing efforts.

Member community business models have evolved over the years from simple advertising models to complex models where members can transact business with each other. In the next chapter, we'll discuss another innovation to the membership model—the flash sales business model.

CHAPTER 14

THE FLASH SALES BUSINESS MODEL

"I don't like those margins. You've got to make it for less."

—Dragon to Pitcher

> **FLASH SALES BUSINESS MODEL**
>
> Pick a niche. Source inventory directly from vendors and manufacturers. License or build an online platform. Launch your model.

Every few years, a new retail model comes along and disrupts an entire industry. In 1881 F.W. Woolworth pioneered the **five-and-dime store** concept after he learned how to set up five-cent tables full of merchandise at his former employer.[1] He went out on his own and realized immediately that he could keep prices cheap by sourcing merchandise directly from factories, instead of through middlemen. His five-cent table concept became the five-and-dime store and his Woolworths stores attracted such a wide audience that they served as the inspiration for careers of retail giants in years to come. S. S. Kresge, Ben Franklin Stores, and even Sam Walton used the five-and-dime-store concept as the foundation for their empires.

Fast-forward to the 1960s. Retail needed a makeover. Sam Walton transformed the course of rural retail by opening up his first Walmart **discount stores**, after cutting his teeth owning several five-and-dime stores. Target came up with a concept called "upscale discount." Kresges was renamed Kmart, and soon after created what looked like an early version of the **flash sales business model,** pioneering a concept called the "Blue Light Special," where a flashing blue light and a well-known announcement—"Attention blue light shoppers!"—caused mini-stampedes throughout the stores. The sales innovation helped Kmart liquidate overstock merchandise during time-limited (sometimes minutes) sales events. If you don't remember the Blue Light Special, you've never shopped at Kmart!

At around the same time, **off-price retail** started catching on with stores like Marshalls and T.J. Maxx. These savvy retail businesses started using an opportunistic buying model to buy and sell brand names at deep discounts. Off-price meant the retailer buys products at prices 25% to 50% below wholesale from retailers looking to liquidate off-season, surplus, and cancelled orders, and pack-and-hold inventory. The low-price buying model allowed savvy businesses to turn around and sell the same merchandise at deep discounts.

Which brings us to today. A world where shoppers can find the lowest prices with the click of the mouse. Entrepreneurs looking to crack into retail on a grand scale today have become highly sophisticated retail buyers, and retail titans are taking notice. In 2001, Vente-privee pioneered the **online flash sales business model** by combining the off-price strategy of a Marshalls (brand names for less) with the time-limited Blue Light Special of Kmart.[2] Jacques-Antoine Granjon figured out a way to bring member-only, time-limited sales events for off-price brands to the Internet. Today the model is all over the Web with flash sales being used to sell clothing, baby products, electronics, and even home décor. In fact, three young entrepreneurs pitched to the Dragons with a flash sales website for furniture and home décor aimed at young professionals who have busy lives and are used to shopping online. And two Dragons with marketing experience liked the model so much that they struck a deal with them.

HOMESAV

Pitchers: Allan Fisch, Aliza Pulver, and Alex Norman, Season 6, Episode 20 (first pitch)

PRODUCT DESCRIPTION

Discount brand-name furniture and home-décor website.

BACKGROUND

The North American home furniture and décor industry is worth $124 billion, 8% of which is online. The three pitchers combine legal, financial, and furniture-industry experience, as well as marketing and buying skills. They saw an opportunity to break into the online marketplace.

PROBLEM STATEMENT

Young professionals want to shop online for furniture and home décor at discount prices.

BUSINESS MODEL

HomeSav is a website that offers deep discounts of up to 70% off retail prices on brand-name home décor and furniture. Members sign up to the website and receive notifications of time-limited sales—HomeSav's flash sales events! When the company receives an order, it sends a purchase order to the relevant supplier. If it is returned, the only risk is the shipping costs—HomeSav carries no inventory risk.

PROOF OF CONCEPT

- **Revenue:** Six months of sales, with last month at $60,000; current year revenue projection is $720,000.
- **Demand:** 25,000 current members.

DRAGONS' DEAL

- **The Ask:** $200,000 for 15% equity.
- **Company Valuation:** $1.33 million.
- **The Deal:** $200,000 for 45% equity.

THE WARM-UP: FLASH SALES BUSINESS MODEL DEFINED

A **flash sales business** holds private, time-limited, member-only daily sales events online for off-price premium brands. The reason flash sales businesses are so popular is because premium brand and artisan manufacturers are given an outlet to liquidate their surplus, closeout, or end-of-season merchandise. The key issues to consider when evaluating whether a flash sales business is right for you are:

- **Revenue Model:** A flash sales business follows an opportunistic buying model to buy and sell off-price brand-name or artisan products that shoppers clamour for. In exchange, the flash sales online business owner earns a gross profit (sometimes 50%) on each item sold, which is used to cover the cost of paying in-house buyers, the online platform, and the operating expenses of the business.

- **Product/Market Focus:** The model works particularly well for surplus, end-of-season, and closeout merchandise (e.g., apparel and accessories) that manufacturers need to liquidate.
- **Value Proposition:** Flash sales events offer the excitement of getting a premium product (brand or artisan) at a deep discount.

Revenue Model: How to Make Money

A flash sales business holds time-limited, member-only sales events online that start and end within 24, 36, or 72 hours. It is essentially a hybrid of the off-price discount concept—for premium brands and artisan products—of a Marshalls or a Winners and the Blue Light Special of a Kmart.

Here's how it works: You source off-price inventory from brands or artisan manufacturers directly or through off-price trade shows—at below wholesale prices. You then set up an online platform for holding 24- to 72-hour sales events. Each sale starts at the same time daily, and is typically member-only to people who have previously signed up to receive daily notifications of your member flash sales events. After a sale closes, you place concrete orders with the brands or artisan manufacturers who have previously agreed to set aside enough inventory for your sale. The product sold gets shipped to your warehouse, and then you ship it to the shoppers so that you retain complete control over the brand experience.

Purchasing inventory like this is opportunistic buying and is a full-time job. If you are buying below wholesale, you can sell at or around wholesale to shoppers, which provides huge value to the shopper. These cyclical, seasonal, and periodic pricing opportunities create a flash sales bonanza for shoppers to buy brand names at deep discounts. The consumer knows that the inventory won't be there tomorrow so they have to buy now. To succeed, you have to know your market and establish trusted relationships with the manufacturers—or you won't have any inventory to sell.

Product/Market Focus: What Sells

There are a few well-known leaders in the flash sales space, including Vente-privee, the European pioneer, and Gilt.[3] Vente-privee started out offering designer clothes, but has since diversified into wine, home appliances, and sports equipment. Fab.com just raised another $105 million.[4] And even Nordstrom is in the market after buying flash sales company HauteLook. But getting into this space might be costly if you don't position your business against the online giants who have had a few years to establish a foothold. The market is becoming controlled by highly skilled retail buyers who use a combination of clout, opportunistic buying, and pack-and-hold strategies to find inventory that online shoppers want.

The key differentiator for this type of business model is the brand-name, luxury, or have-to-have merchandise being sold. The flash sales business model works for branded products that people immediately understand the value of because they need to make quick decisions. To help you come up with your own flash sales business model, consider some of the more popular product/market themes, and then consider combining or adjusting them with artisan, niche (e.g., women or college students), local, or other themes.

Flash Sales Theme	Description
End-of-Season Merchandise	Items that are no longer in season and that will be out of fashion by next season, such as apparel or shoes. Manufacturers (brand name or artisan) have to monetize excess stock to free up cash for next season.
Limited-Shelf-Life Merchandise	Perishable items like packaged gift food items or travel packages that manufacturers or service providers have to sell or the items lose value.
Niche Merchandise	Items that are designed for a specific target customer such as babies, moms, or men. Zulily sells to goods for moms, babies, and kids, while Jack Threads sells to men.
Overstock Items Merchandise	Items that manufacturers have overrun and need to liquidate in a short period of time. Manufacturers need to monetize items that might go off trend next year, so they are willing to sell them to flash sales online retailers.

Value Proposition: Why It Works

Prior to the wave of off-price email offers that we've all become used to, surplus inventory was liquidated through brick-and-mortar off-price retailers like Winners, Marshalls, and T.J. Maxx. Today off-price merchandise is available through daily deals websites like Groupon, Overstock.com, and of course flash sales websites like Gilt and Vente-privee. The value proposition of this business model includes:

- **Inventory Management:** The flash sales business model is a liquidation solution for brand-name or luxury retailers and manufacturers that have surplus or closeout inventory. The flash sales business acts as a sales channel for items that need to be liquidated to make room for new inventory.

- **Impulse Buying:** Flash sales lead to unplanned purchases because shoppers feel they are getting a deal on something that won't be available for long.
- **Off-Price Retail:** Flash sales attract impulse buyers who are looking for deep discounts on luxury or off-price items that they normally wouldn't buy.
- **Sense of Urgency:** Because all flash sales are time limited, not volume limited like those found on deal-of-the-day sites like Groupon, customers feel pressure to make a quick decision.
- **Transition Business Model:** The flash sales business model is ideal for entrepreneurs who are looking to establish a more traditional purchasing model, by establishing a foothold in a niche.
- **Why It's Disruptive:** This method of doing business is a novelty for people who are used to traditional purchasing models found on fixed-price websites.

DRAGON LORE

A buying opportunity for flash sales business model entrepreneurs is an end-of-season, overrun, or business-closure sale of inventory that needs to be converted into cash fast.

So how can bricks-and-mortar retail compete against pricing innovations like this? Two young entrepreneurs came to the Dragons' Den with their solution, MappedIn. They had come up with an idea to solve a simple problem—the static analog mall directory. And they've not only gained traction with real paying customers, but they also managed to convince every Dragon to want in on the deal.

MAPPEDIN

Pitchers: Hongwei Liu and Desmond Choi, Season 7, Episode 6
PRODUCT DESCRIPTION

Interactive touch-screen mall directory kiosk and smartphone app for point-to-point directions in malls.

BACKGROUND

Hongwei Liu and Desmond Choi both started businesses when they were very young, and brought that experience to MappedIn. MappedIn is one of those software solutions that makes you wonder why someone else hasn't done it already. The two pitchers managed to secure three contracts in only one month of being in business by giving shoppers a way to navigate the mall with a smartphone app.

PROBLEM STATEMENT

Many of us have used GPS in our cars, but when we get to a mall, we still use an alphanumeric board map to navigate and find stores.

BUSINESS MODEL

MappedIn leases interactive touch-screen directories to malls for a fee of $5,000 per month. They complement the solution with a free smartphone app that gives shoppers point-to-point directions in the mall. Shoppers can use the directory and the free smartphone app to find what they are looking for, including sales. And stores can use the system to push messages about in-store specials to shoppers who are using the smartphone app.

PROOF OF CONCEPT

- **Revenue:** $120,000 in revenue in one month of business. Projected revenue this year is $1 million.
- **Distribution:** Three contracts secured so far.

DRAGONS' DEAL

- **The Ask:** $150,000 for 10% equity.
- **Company Valuation:** $1.5 million.
- **The Deal:** $375,000 for 25% equity with three Dragons in on the deal, including a digital pioneer, a disciplined financial investor, and a restaurant industry giant.

START-UP ESSENTIALS: Flash Sales Business Model

1. Pick a **theme** for your business, such as moms, babies, artisan, or brand products.
2. **Source inventory** directly from vendors and manufacturers.

3. Buy, build, or license an **online platform.**

4. Create a **smartphone app** so members can track sales, since many orders will be placed by shoppers on smartphones.

5. Incorporate social media tools that allow **sign-in** using Facebook or Twitter logins.

PART IV SELF-STUDY WORKSHOP

At the heart of a membership business model is repeat revenue. Having a subscription fee coming in every month can prevent you from having to re-establish new business after every sale. In this workshop, try to think of as many creative ways as possible that you can charge for your products or services. Then discuss how your operating process is set up to handle growth in customers over time.

ESTABLISH A REPEAT REVENUE MODEL

1. Who **pays you?**
   - ❏ Consumer
   - ❏ Business
   - ❏ Professional
   - ❏ Middleman (e.g., licensee, franchisee)
   - ❏ Other

2. How does your product or service **generate revenue?**

3. How do you **charge** for each of the things that you do?
   - ❏ Product revenue (unit price)
   - ❏ Service fee
   - ❏ Transaction fee
   - ❏ Licensing fee
   - ❏ Royalty fee
   - ❏ Franchising fee
   - ❏ Other

4. When do you **get paid?** How do you **collect?**
    - ❑ Up front
    - ❑ Installment payments
    - ❑ Milestone payments
    - ❑ Back end
    - ❑ Other

5. Is your revenue model **scalable?** Can you respond to sudden increases in sales volume without spreading your staff and financial resources thin?

6. What is your **pricing model?**
    - **Price Floor:** What is the lowest price you could charge and still generate a profit?
    - **Price Ceiling:** What is the highest price you could charge and still have customers willing to pay you?
    - **Price Point:** What price point will generate the highest number of customers?

7. What is the **lifetime value of each customer?** (annual revenue × the number of years a customer will pay you, in today's dollars)

In this chapter, we discussed the flash sales business model. The strength behind this model is the combination of off-price products and time-limited, private selling events. In the next chapter, we'll discuss how to tap into the power of crowds of individuals—crowdsourcing business models.

PART V

CROWDSOURCING BUSINESS MODELS

Launch a business model that taps into the collective power of individuals who want to help complete online tasks, fund causes, and share underutilized assets.

CHAPTER 15

THE CROWDSOURCING BUSINESS MODEL

"A vision without execution is nothing."

—Dragon to Pitcher

CROWDSOURCING BUSINESS MODEL

Determine the tasks you would like to help crowdsource. Build or license an online platform. Soft launch your model with tasks from family, friends, and colleagues. Then hard launch your business with a full-scale marketing campaign.

Many highly skilled individuals have time outside of their daily jobs to do freelance work on the side. There are also many entities that would be willing to pay those people for their skills if they were just able to find them. Unfortunately these two entities often never meet because of something called "frictional unemployment." Frictional unemployment is a type of unemployment where individuals with skills can't find the entities that have the need for those skills because of the costs and benefits involved in the process. If those two entities were just able to find each other somehow, then a match would be made, the individual would no longer be unemployed, and the entity would have its task completed.

That's where **crowdsourcing** comes in. The crowdsourcing business model capitalizes on the skills of pockets of individuals in remote areas, who can complete online tasks. The term was popularized by Jeff Howe in his book *Crowdsourcing: Why the Power of the Crowd Is Driving the Future of Business.*[1] It shouldn't be confused with a similar term—**user-generated content.** User-generated content is just that—content that is posted by an individual visitor to a website. Crowdsourcing, on the other hand, uses collective knowledge and effort to build a valuable solution, such as a video, a logo, a cure, or maybe even a consumer product.

Now what if you could crowdsource a resolution to the Arab-Israeli conflict? That's what Yaron Bazaz thought was possible when he visited *Dragons' Den*. He had an online crowdsourcing idea called CrowdFanatic, which is a platform where crowds can confront crowds over topics of debate. His business roadmap included crowdvoting, advertising, and affinity group–targeted merchandise sales. However, a vision is not a business, so he had a hard time pitching his concept. And he, like some pitchers who visit the Dragons' Den with only an idea and nothing more, was skewered by the Dragons. On a good note, his idea is actually becoming somewhat popular today. Today, Deeyoon is a website where individuals can debate each other one-on-one live on webcams, while others vote on who they think won the debate. And ConvinceMe allows individuals to argue online over any topic with another individual, while others voice their opinion on which side they favour. So maybe Yaron Bazaz should retool and return to the Den.

CROWDFANATIC

Pitcher: Yaron Bazaz, Season 3, Episode 6

PRODUCT DESCRIPTION

A website called CrowdFanatic where groups can debate issues and further their own agendas.

BACKGROUND

Yaron Bazaz wanted to help crowds settle their disputes online where the chance of physical confrontation is zero. He came to the Den hoping that the Dragons would help him, but unfortunately the Dragons had other thoughts.

PROBLEM STATEMENT

How to confront a rival group online.

BUSINESS MODEL

A groups-versus-groups voting platform where rival crowds confront each other over a specific debating point, aiming directly to sway each other's opinions. The firm plans to offer memorabilia, merchandise, and other items that appeal to users' specific interests.

PROOF OF CONCEPT

- **Capacity:** The concept was unproven prior to visiting the Dragons' Den.

DRAGONS' DEAL

- **The Ask:** $500,000 for 10% equity.
- **Company Valuation:** $5,000,000.
- **The Deal:** $0 because the company was pre-revenue and did not have a site up and running when they came on the show.

THE WARM-UP: CROWDSOURCING BUSINESS MODEL DEFINED

Crowdsourcing is a business model where a number of remote individuals help complete a task that is posted online. It's an outsource-to-anybody business model. The reason crowdsourcing is so popular is because it allows a crowd of people to collectively design a logo, come up with a product idea, build an online map, or help complete an online project all while competing for a "bounty" in an open forum. To evaluate whether crowdsourcing is right for you, consider:

- **Revenue Model:** Crowdsourcing websites typically charge a transaction fee against a bounty that has been put up to attract people to help solve the problem or complete the task.
- **Product/Market Focus:** The crowdsourcing model works best for digital tasks that can be completed online, such as logo design or data mapping.
- **Value Proposition:** Crowdsourcing can lead to superior outcomes at lower costs.

Revenue Model: How to Make Money

When you start a crowdsourcing business, you are in the business of helping people complete online tasks and projects by connecting them with an on-demand workforce. In exchange, you receive a transaction fee or shared bounty for the work that is completed through your platform. This business model takes the concept of matching one step further because the platform actually helps people complete the task.

Here's how it works: This is an outsource-to-anybody business model. You build a platform where entities in need of a workforce can post a project for something like a logo or video. These entities agree to pay a **bounty** to the person who finishes the job to their satisfaction. You then market those tasks to people who have the skills to complete those tasks. There needs to be little or no intervention between the entities who want a specific task to be completed, and the crowds of people who have the skills to do the work. To the entity in need of the work, it will feel like Adam Smith's "invisible hand" at work because all kinds of sample solutions will start showing up in their inboxes. The revenue models that are used to monetize the process include:

- **Bounty:** The entity in need of work puts up a bounty and rewards it to the individual service provider who does the best job on the task. You then share the fee with that person.
- **Service Fee:** Charge a fee to facilitate completion of the work and share that fee with the freelancer.
- **Transaction Fee:** Charge a transaction fee against any fee agreed to between the freelancer and the entity in need of work.

Product/Market Focus: What Sells

The crowdsourcing business model has proven to be quite popular among investors and end-users. Investors funded 99designs with $35 million in 2011 for its crowdsourcing website.[2] Investors also funded Poptent with $5.5 million in 2012.[3] So the next time you need a logo, a video, a task completed, or just about any problem solved, consider a business model that taps into the collective knowledge and expertise of crowds of people. Or consider *integrating* crowdsourcing into your business model. You might just get funded by a Dragon. Here are some popular crowdsourcing models:

Business Model Theme	Description
Design Tournaments	A business model you set up where businesses request a logo design, and have designers compete for a bounty against each other in an open forum. The designers can see each other's work, as can the people requesting it. (E.g., 99designs.)
Merchandising Tournaments	A business model you set up where merchandisers crowdsource ideas on what to produce/sell on their websites. Have site members/visitors vote on the best designs and then create inventory to sell, based on those votes. (E.g., Threadless.)
Tutoring Model	A business model you set up where students ask a question to a "crowd" of tutors and receive written answers back from those tutors who have an answer. The student then previews each answer and chooses the best one in exchange for a fee. (E.g., Student of Fortune.)
Task Model	A business model you set up where individuals or entities issue invitations to freelancers to complete a specific, definable task (e.g., errands, research, phone calls) or scopeable project (e.g., website development, resumé). The freelancer who has the best price and plan for the work wins the project and gets paid when the work is complete. (E.g., TaskRabbit or CrowdSource.)
Product Testing	A business model you set up where entities have their software or products tested by crowds of users. (E.g., uTest.)
Data Gathering	A business model where an entity sources location statistics from the crowd based on a common factor, such as people who have a specific illness, in order to build data maps. (E.g., Flu Near You.)

Value Proposition: Why It Works

Crowdsourcing is popular because it distributes work to a location-agnostic workforce of individuals. The deliverables are often superior to what would be provided by commercial businesses because the work is completed in an open forum where freelancers can collaborate and see each other's work. Assuming iron sharpens iron, the feature of being able to see each other's work helps to improve the end result. The value proposition of this business model includes:

- **On-Demand Skills:** People can outsource a task through an open call to a crowd of freelancers who are often highly skilled and underutilized workers with free time. The freelancers then compete for your business in an open forum, often driving down prices and improving outcomes.

- **Collaboration:** When a problem or task is being tackled by multiple people in an open forum, a superior result can occur because more eyes are on the project.
- **Collective Wisdom:** Large groups of people can help iterate a solution faster in an open forum than individuals can on their own privately.
- **Downward Pricing Pressure:** Crowds competing for the business of one entity drive down prices while improving outcomes.
- **Research:** Unsolved problems can be used to solve problems in a collaborative environment.
- **Why it's disruptive:** Crowdsourcing is disruptive because it facilitates a large number of micro donations from a geographically dispersed group of donors.

DRAGON LORE

Crowdsourcing works best when you offer a bounty to anyone who helps to complete the task.

Sometimes a business uses a hybrid of multiple business models to achieve its revenue targets. For example, Ethical Ocean is a marketplace where ethical-product sellers post fair trade and eco-friendly products for sale. The Ethical Ocean team then **crowdsources** the task of figuring out which products are ethical and which ones are not through its online community. The Ethical Ocean team then makes a final decision as to which products are not ethical. They look for sellers who sell animal-friendly, people-friendly, or environment-friendly products and remove the ones that the community feels are not ethical. They also offer **crowdfunding** (through a relationship with FlipGive) to help Ethical Ocean community members raise money for fundraisers. After being called "a stain on the face of capitalism" by one of the Dragons, the company seems to be thriving in the world of ethical consumption.

ETHICAL OCEAN

Pitchers: Tony Hancock and David Damberger, Season 5, Episode 20
PRODUCT DESCRIPTION
An online ethical-products marketplace.

BACKGROUND

The pitchers were looking to participate in an ethical-products market that they say is worth $40 billion dollars and is growing at a rate of 15% annually. So they launched an ethical-products marketplace where ethical-product sellers can market their products to end consumers, and consumers can be sure that they are buying ethical products.

PROBLEM STATEMENT

Where to buy fair trade, organic, and sweatshop-free products.

BUSINESS MODEL

Crowdsources ethical products from ethical sellers across North America, and allows them to sell directly to consumers. Community members report unethical products and the products are removed instantly.

PROOF OF CONCEPT

- **Revenue:** Sold $1,000 in products in week one, and $4,000 in week two.
- **Distribution:** 100 product sellers have loaded products on the site in the last two months.
- **Traffic:** 15,000 visitors to the site so far.

DRAGONS' DEAL

- **The Ask:** $150,000 for 20% equity.
- **Company Valuation:** $750,000.
- **The Deal:** $150,000 for 20% equity from one Dragon who brings marketing experience to the deal.

START-UP ESSENTIALS: Crowdsourcing Business Model

1. Determine **the types of tasks** that your online platform will crowdsource.
2. Determine the **deliverables** that your online platform will store (e.g., logo designs, product theme songs, digital documents, task plans).
3. Choose a **revenue source** such as a transaction fee or a bounty.
4. Build or license a **crowdsourcing platform.**

5. Set up a **payment-processing** method so freelancers can get paid in a timely manner.

6. Create a free **mobile app** so freelancers can track their tasks and so employers can track deliverables.

Crowdsourcing proves that individuals can be mobilized to achieve tasks, complete projects, and drive down costs. And if you can figure out how to build a platform that helps people crowdsource their work, you can build a healthy business. In the next chapter, we'll talk about another model that mobilizes crowds to achieve goals—the crowdfunding business model.

CHAPTER 16

THE CROWDFUNDING BUSINESS MODEL

"The future of business is to be socially responsible, environmentally friendly, and [to] make money."

—Dragon to Pitcher

> **CROWDFUNDING BUSINESS MODEL**
>
> Choose a theme for your crowdfunding model. Build a crowdfunding platform or license a white-label solution. Launch your model and build a user base.

There is nothing new about **crowdfunding.** Just look back in history and you'll find numerous examples of people engaging the crowd in order to achieve financial goals. Susan G. Komen's sister, Nancy Goodman Brinker, mobilized millions to support the search for a cure for breast cancer with what is now the famous pink-ribbon campaign. Lance Armstrong established the Livestrong Foundation and also mobilized millions to find a cure for cancer. Millard and Linda Fuller mobilized millions to build houses for people in need when they established Habitat for Humanity. And when it comes to fundraising to fund a cause using the crowd, look no further than the Jerry Lewis Telethon that used to occupy our Labour Day weekends. Jerry Lewis was the grandfather of fundraising. He would set a fundraising target, bring in celebrities who donated their time to entertain the crowd, and the crowd would pledge money and watch the famous "tote board" go up over the weekend. Then at the end of the telethon, the final funding tally would be announced, and the funds disbursed to help cure muscular dystrophy.

Today celebrities have been replaced by relatively unknown individuals with computers. The television audience has been replaced by your own personal social network on Facebook, LinkedIn, and Twitter, and your email contact list. The telephone has been replaced by a web app that lets your crowd make donations completely online. And the name telethon has been replaced by a more cutting-edge term—"crowdfunding." But the spirit of the model is relatively unchanged. Crowdfunding is an online mini-telethon that individuals set up to fund a specific cause that interests them. It taps into the power of a crowd, which is no more than a group of individuals with a shared interest, who pledge money for a cause, project, or business investment. It's a do-it-yourself online fundraising service established by savvy entrepreneurs who get paid a transaction fee on the amounts raised. Today, there are tens of thousands of mini-fundraisers being held online, all sourcing the crowd to get money for their causes, start-ups, and projects.

There are few places more active in fundraising than your child's school. Schools have to raise money, and there are crowds of parents dropping their kids off there every day who are willing to donate funds to make their kid's school a better place. Entrepreneur Darryl Davis from Wealthy School Revolution doesn't use a crowdfunding model—yet. But he does tap into the collective resources of a crowd using an online platform. And his funding platform works so well that two Dragons jumped at the deal.

WEALTHY SCHOOL REVOLUTION

Pitcher: Darryl Davis, Season 7, Episode 5

PRODUCT DESCRIPTION

An online fundraising platform that enables school PAC committees to offer useful, everyday consumer products to parents. Participating schools receive a commission from Wealthy School Revolution on every item sold.

BACKGROUND[1]

There are 16,000 schools in Canada and 150,000 in North America. Every school in North America is fundraising, and traditional funding sources aren't proving effective.

PROBLEM STATEMENT

School fundraisers evoke negative emotions because parents are being bombarded with solicitations for money.

BUSINESS MODEL

Wealthy School Revolution provides a free online school fundraising platform to parent volunteers, offering useful products for parents to buy and pick up at school. Wealthy School Revolution makes a 35% profit margin on all the products sold, and provides 10% of every sale to the fundraising school.

PROOF OF CONCEPT

- **Revenue:** Sales to date are $110,000 on groceries alone.
- **Distribution:** WSR has 100 schools in B.C. registered in the program. Each order period, they ship to 40 different schools.
- **Demand:** 95% of schools that hear about Wealthy School Revolution through word-of-mouth advertising and site visits sign up for the program.

DRAGONS' DEAL

- **The Ask:** $300,000 for 25% equity.
- **Company Valuation:** $1.2 million.
- **The Deal:** $300,000 for 25% equity, as requested.

THE WARM-UP: CROWDFUNDING BUSINESS MODEL DEFINED

A **crowdfunding business** provides an online platform for individuals to hold fundraisers and solicit donations from their social networks (Facebook, LinkedIn, Twitter) in exchange for a transaction fee against all funds raised. The reason crowdfunding businesses are so popular is because once you build a platform, you receive transaction fees for matching fundraisers with donors (or investors in the future) from their social networks. For individuals, it's a trusted and socially acceptable way to solicit donations from people they know. The key issues to consider when evaluating whether a crowdfunding business model is right for you are:

- **Revenue Model:** You charge a transaction fee (4% to 10%) against all funds raised by each individual who holds a fundraiser on your platform.
- **Product/Market Focus:** The model works particularly well for individual fundraising events that support social causes, personal pleas for help, and start-up funding.
- **Value Proposition:** Individual fundraisers are given access to a turnkey payment processing method, campaign-building tools, and social network sharing tools to build and share online fundraising campaigns in minutes.

Revenue Model: How to Make Money

When you start a crowdfunding business, you are in the business of facilitating peer-to-peer fundraising campaigns and processing donations for small individual fundraisers. In exchange, you are paid a transaction fee of 4% to 10% (or whatever you decide) of each project's fundraising total. Essentially, you are providing a sophisticated webpage-building solution with fundraising features such as the ability to accept donations, process payments, stay compliant with securities regulators, and share campaigns with social networks.

Here's how it works: Individual fundraisers log in to a website that you build. They can then set up a fundraising-campaign webpage, complete with a fundraising goal and time frame. Individual fundraisers are people who have a social, personal, or business cause that they need funded, such as a renewable energy project, a medical bill, or a start-up business. Fundraisers then market their campaigns themselves to their own personal social networks. Ideally, they'll need an established social network of at least 200 people in order to gain traction from their social networking efforts. Donors are charged nothing other than the money they pledge. When the predefined project funding goal has been met, the money is distributed to the fundraiser and your business collects a percentage of those fees. As the entrepreneur who runs the platform, you have complete control over the community-wide terms of the fundraisers you facilitate. Terms you set for the community might include provision points that state when funds are released to the fundraiser (e.g., does the fundraiser have to raise all funds requested before they are released or does the fundraiser get the funds even if only a percentage of the goal is raised?). There are three current operating models to consider:

- **Donations-Based Models:** Individual fundraisers post social or personal cause projects with specific funding goals. Donors receive nothing in return other than the personal satisfaction of being involved in a project that interests them.

- **Perks Models:** Individual fundraisers post projects with specific funding goals. Donors receive perks from the individuals holding them, such as product samples in exchange for their donation. No equity is traded or offered, so this model can avoid the securities regulation complications involved with equity-based models.

- **Equity-Based Models:** Fundraisers post start-up details and funding goals. Investors receive an equity stake in return for the investment made on the fundraiser's campaign page. In most cases, this model is not yet legal if individual fundraisers are soliciting investments from unaccredited investors. Models for accredited investors are currently in business and regulations for non-accredited investor equity-based models are pending.[2] To build your online platform, you can hire a web-development firm, program it yourself if you are a web developer, or pay a monthly fee (a few hundred dollars a month) for a white-label solution such as Launcht, where you just add your logo to a software-as-a-service website. You'll also need to establish a relationship with a payment-processing firm, such as PayPal, that may take 3% to 5% of each project's total funding, in addition to your own transaction fee. Because no inventory is required and no warehouse is needed to store goods, crowdfunding is a highly scalable business model.

Product/Market Focus: What Sells

The crowdfunding business model is attracting major angel and venture capital investments. Indiegogo raised $15 million in Series A financing in 2012 after facilitating over 100,000 fundraising campaigns. Kickstarter raised $10 million in 2011, with over 33,000 projects funded. And securities regulators such as the OSC in Ontario, and the SEC in the United States, are probing whether and how to make an equity-based model legal going forward so that start-ups can crowdfund their business in exchange for micro-shares.

The most successful crowdfunding businesses focus on causes, projects, or start-up ventures that appeal to affinity groups and personal social networks. With typical funding amounts raised being in the $2,000 range, this is a very attractive service for people looking to fund a project quickly. For example, a small cupcake business called Robicelli's raised $8,755 on Indiegogo to pay for a refrigerated bakery case, building materials, and contractors to finish their build-out.[3] All they provided in exchange was free cupcakes. To help you come up with your own crowdfunding business model, consider some of the more popular product/market themes:

Crowdfunding Theme	Description
Social-Cause Fundraising	Help individuals raise money for a charity, renewable-energy project, school, or social-entrepreneurship start-up. For example, CauseVox holds social-cause fundraisers and charges 7.5% of the amount raised to everyone, plus a monthly membership fee to those who raise $3,000 or more.
Personal-Cause Funding	Help individuals raise funds to pay personal bills, including medical bills, weddings, storm damage, or even education. For example, GoFundMe helps people raise funds for these activities and charges 5% of each donation the fundraiser receives.
Entertainment-Project Funding	Help entertainment-industry participants raise funds for entertainment projects. For example, Kickstarter helps people raise funds for projects such as games or independent films. Kickstarter charges 5% of the project's total funding and third-party payment processors charge 3% to 5% of the funds raised.
Business-Project or Start-Up Funding	Help individuals raise rounds of seed or series funding to start a business or fund an innovative product. For example, Fundable allows entrepreneurs to pitch accredited investors by uploading their pitch documents. Currently only accredited investors can receive equity in exchange. All others receive product rewards for what is termed their donation. Fundable charges $99 per month while you are trying to raise funds, and a third-party payment processor receives 3.5% of any funds raised.

Value Proposition: Why It Works

Crowdfunding is popular because it enables a large number of small-dollar donors to participate in projects or causes they otherwise would never have heard of. It also allows fundraisers to overcome fundraising challenges by tapping into the collective resources of everyday individuals with a platform that is less socially awkward than a verbal solicitation for funds. If you are a budding entrepreneur with technical skills or access to them, it allows you to generate small-percentage, high-volume transaction fees in exchange for providing a platform that connects individual fundraisers with donors. The value proposition of this business model includes:

- **Transaction Fees:** The entrepreneur who sets up the fundraising platform receives transaction fees (4% to 10% of total dollars raised) from each campaign that is held.
- **Collectivism:** Fundraisers achieve fundraising goals by using the collective power of their social networks.

- **Low-Cost Fundraising:** Crowdfunding allows individuals to fundraise using low-cost marketing through their own email contact databases or no-cost social networks such as Facebook, Twitter, LinkedIn, Foursquare, or Pinterest.
- **Payment Processing and Compliance:** Crowdfunding services provide payment processing so individuals don't have to worry about collecting and managing cash. You also provide securities regulation compliance assistance that most individual fundraisers would not be able to afford.
- **User-Generated Content:** Individual fundraisers, who are the customers of the business, generate all of the content on your fundraising platform. They create the campaigns, come up with goals, and market the campaigns themselves, with their own social networks.
- **Social Value:** Causes, projects, and start-ups that might otherwise never have been funded are being funded. Donors get to participate with small dollar amounts in many different causes that appeal to them. Fundraisers get support for their own fundraising causes or passions.
- **Why It's Disruptive:** Crowdfunding uses the power of peer-to-peer transactions and social networking to mobilize a large number of otherwise inactive low-dollar donors and investors. In the past, it was not cost effective to market to low-dollar donors in remote locations.

DRAGON LORE

The most successful individual fundraising projects are driven by social media campaigns that the fundraisers themselves initiate through their own social networks, including Facebook, LinkedIn, or their email contact database. Encourage fundraisers to build their own personal social networks up to a minimum of 200 people or more before launching their individual fundraisers.

When Bradley Friesen pitched his proprietary hangover cure and patented cap and bottle system to the Dragons, his colourful personality had all five Dragons engaged. They not only saw the value of the product as is, but also the licensing potential for the cap and bottle technology. Since he visited the Den, Last Call has raised capital via crowdsourcing website Indiegogo. Indiegogo lists Last Call as one of their favourite pitches.[4]

LAST CALL

Pitcher: Bradley Friesen, Season 6, Episode 20

PRODUCT DESCRIPTION

A hangover-prevention drink.

BACKGROUND

Before pitcher Bradley Friesen got laid off, he worked in the plastics business in injection moulding. He developed and patented a cap and bottle system that keeps powder in a bottle cap until it is twisted, when it is delivered into water. Last Call is a proprietary hangover cure comprising electrolytes, potassium, sodium, melatonin, dehydrated ginger, and Vitamins B and C.

PROBLEM STATEMENT

Everyone likes to party, but no one likes the hangover the next day.

BUSINESS MODEL

Friesen plans to sell Last Call through bars and nightclubs. The patented cap and bottle delivery system has the potential for licensing for other products and uses.

PROOF OF CONCEPT

- **Revenue:** No sales at the time of the pitch.

DRAGONS' DEAL

- **The Ask:** $5,000 for 5% equity.
- **Company Valuation:** $100,000.
- **The Deal:** $25,000 for 10% of the company from all five Dragons.

START-UP ESSENTIALS: Crowdfunding Business Model

1. **Establish a theme** for your crowdfunding, such as social causes, personal needs, or start-up funding.

2. **Research competitor models** online for transaction fee structures, community rules, and marketing methods.

3. Speak with a lawyer who can help you map out a **user agreement** that contains community-wide rules, including transaction fees, for your users' fundraisers.

4. Speak with an insurance expert about the types of **liability insurance** you will need to protect your crowdfunding business from unscrupulous fundraisers who try to take advantage of donors with fake campaigns.

5. Establish a relationship with a **payment processor** such as PayPal, Square, or Amazon payments.

6. Buy, build, or lease a white-label solution to act as your **web platform** to enable others to crowdfund their projects online.

Even the crowdfunding industry is getting crowded with new competitors. As in all industries, the best way to enter an overcrowded market is to have a strong differentiator. Types of projects funded include social entrepreneurship, film projects, consumer-product start-ups, retail-outlet start-ups, charity, and even personal medical bills. Most models as of this writing are donation models, with the donor of the funds receiving nothing in return. But the future will include investment returns for business start-ups that offer shares, as securities regulators in various jurisdictions figure out a way to regulate high-quantity, low-dollar investments from unaccredited investors. In the next chapter, we'll discuss another business model that taps into the compelling need that individuals have to do business with each other—peer-to-peer sharing.

CHAPTER 17

THE PEER-TO-PEER SHARING BUSINESS MODEL

"I love you two guys. I love investing with smart people."

—Dragon to Pitcher

> **PEER-TO-PEER SHARING BUSINESS MODEL**
>
> Identify the property that will be shared. Build an online or wired platform that enables peer-to-peer sharing. Launch your model using a city-by-city roll-out strategy.

Back in 1918, 10 years after Henry Ford stormed the world with his car-for-everyone strategy, Walter L. Jacobs saw an opportunity. People were arriving at destinations and needed more flexible transportation options. So he purchased a fleet of Model Ts and pioneered a drive-yourself system. He would share his fleet of cars, for a fee, with anyone who wanted one, as long as they agreed to return it within a set period of time. Five years later he cashed out and his system was officially branded as the "Hertz Drive-Ur-Self System."[1]

Over 90 years later, thanks to the Internet, we are still renting cars and driving ourselves—but now it's in other people's cars too. Individuals like you and me are now renting cars to each other. And we're not only driving ourselves, we're doing the paperwork, negotiating the rental fees, and parking the cars. The process is called **peer-to-peer sharing** and has its technological roots back in 1999 when a popular yet controversial service called "Napster" came on the scene. Napster was a software program that made music files on one computer visible and shareable with someone on another computer. When you take that networking power one step further, you realize that the Internet allows the needs of one individual to be visible and shareable with those of other individuals, and that's why it's called "peer-to-peer sharing."

That ability of the Internet to connect two geographically dispersed individuals who share the same interests is now the basis for a whole range of sharing business models. Airbnb connects individuals who want to share their unused homes, with other individuals. Getaround connects people who want to share their unused cars. And *Dragons' Den* veteran NoteWagon connects students who want to share their school notes with other students. You can share just about anything for a fee: an empty home, an unused vehicle, an underutilized asset, or even school notes, as NoteWagon is proving.

NOTEWAGON

Pitchers: Saif Altimimi and Shawn Swartman, Season 6, Episode 6

PRODUCT DESCRIPTION

A peer-to-peer note-sharing website where university and college students share student notes.

BACKGROUND

Saif was looking for a way to capitalize on the underground note-sharing ecosystem that was already occurring in schools. Students were sharing study guides and chapter summaries, but no one was facilitating the process online. So he built an online platform where students could interact with each other, and earn money in the process.

PROBLEM STATEMENT

Students who miss a class because of illness, work, or extracurricular activities need a better system for staying up-to-date with missed classes.

BUSINESS MODEL

An online document-sharing platform where students can upload class notes for other students to buy from them. Students buy tokens, which are then exchanged for cash, and the company makes money by charging a 50% fee against the dollar amount of tokens that exchange hands. The notes can be resold over and over again, which makes this model a repeat-revenue model.

PROOF OF CONCEPT

- **Funding:** The company had already raised a round of funding at a $500,000 valuation.
- **Demand:** Gained 15,000 users in the six weeks leading up to the show.

DRAGONS' DEAL

- **The Ask:** $200,000 for 20% equity.
- **Company Valuation:** $1,000,000.
- **The Deal:** $250,000 for 32.5% equity with all five Dragons in on the deal.

THE WARM-UP: PEER-TO-PEER SHARING BUSINESS MODEL DEFINED

A **peer-to-peer sharing business** provides an online platform where individuals can share their personal property with other individuals in exchange for a transaction fee against all fees charged by sharers. The reason peer-to-peer sharing businesses are so popular is that individuals are given the opportunity to monetize property that would otherwise just sit idle for part of the day or month. The key issues to consider when evaluating whether a peer-to-peer sharing business model is right for you are:

- **Revenue Model:** The individuals who share property charge a below-market fee to each other for that right. As the entrepreneur who sets up the platform, you keep a percentage of the transaction, ranging from 40% for cars or 6% to 12% for housing.
- **Product/Market Focus:** This business model works best for sharing property that takes a significant amount of capital to buy outright (with the exception of digital-sharing businesses such as NoteWagon).
- **Value Proposition:** You help people monetize their underutilized personal and real property.

Revenue Model: How to Make Money

When you start a peer-to-peer sharing business, you are in the business of connecting individual property owners with other individuals who want to rent from them, facilitating payments, and building trust between the individuals. In exchange for facilitating payments and the trust-building services you provide (e.g., screening) between the two parties, you receive a transaction fee of 3% to 40% of whatever money changes hands (or whatever fee your market will bear).

Here's how it works: This is a "share your stuff with a stranger for a fee" model. You are providing a sharing platform online where individuals can share items with trusted individuals that your business has pre-qualified and vetted. You are also providing a social-networking structure where connections can be made with individuals who the sharer might otherwise have never met. As the organizer and intermediary, you receive a transaction fee for any sharing that you facilitate and, in some cases, you screen the people sharing. A transaction fee can range from a low fee, such as 3% for simple items like digital items, to a higher fee, like 40% for more sophisticated property like cars. Most peer-to-peer sharing platforms also provide a *complementary* smartphone app that mirrors the web interface. Smartphone apps are critical to a service like this because they allow potential renters to find the items being shared using GPS. There are two operating models to consider:

- **Public Model:** For a transaction fee based on the rental fee that individuals pay each other, you screen potential renters and letters, then allow them to post what they want to share. People then share with anyone who has been screened by your online platform.
- **Invite-Only Model:** For a transaction fee based on the rental fee that individuals pay each other, individuals screen each other themselves. You enable others to build private sharing groups so people can share with friends.

Product/Market Focus: What Sells

You know a business model is powerful when it attracts the attention of Google and General Motors. Since its inception in 2011, RelayRides, a car-sharing business, has attracted over $13 million in funding from venture capital firms including Google Ventures and General Motors Ventures.[2] Airbnb, a home-sharing service, has attracted over $100 million in venture funding since its inception in 2008. And Skillshare, a website where people can offer courses to others, has attracted over $3 million in venture funding.

The key differentiator for this type of business model is the type of property that is being shared. To succeed in this space, entrepreneurs focus on creating platforms that enable sharing of items that are insurable, trackable, and require a significant amount of capital to purchase outright. To help you come up with your own peer-to-peer sharing business model, consider some of the more popular product/market themes:

Peer-to-Peer Sharing Model	Description
Personal Property Sharing	Enable individuals to rent their personal property to other individuals. Works with cars, bikes, and other items of value that are insurable. Companies like Getaround and RelayRides charge a 40% commission to the owner of the rental property against a daily rental rate set by the owner. Rental-rate models include booking fees, plus a variety of other late fees, citation fees, and administration fees.
Real Estate Sharing	Enable others to share their real estate property with other individuals. Works with unused homes, vacation property, office space, or gardens. Companies like Airbnb charge service fees to the guest (e.g., 6% to 12% of reservation total) plus booking fees to the host property owner (e.g., 3% of reservation total).
Knowledge Sharing	Enable others to share their skills, intellectual property, or even notes with other individuals. Companies like Skillshare give people the tools they need to teach, to design classes, and to sell tickets online. Skillshare keeps a transaction fee of 15% of all revenue from tickets sold.
Ride Sharing	Enable others to share rides and receive a payment for sharing extra space in their cars. For example, companies like Zimride or Sidecar enable ride sharing and allow for voluntary donations (e.g., chip in for gas) to keep local taxi or limo regulations at bay.
Local Neighbourhood Sharing	Enable others to set up a private network with close friends and neighbours with whom you share your goods, at no cost. Companies like Neighborgoods facilitate neighbour-to-neighbour sharing using an online platform.

Value Proposition: Why It Works

Peer-to-peer sharing business models are popular because assets such as vacation property and vehicles are often grossly underutilized. Many people would love to monetize those assets, but lack the social connections required to find remote strangers who would be willing to pay them. The market has lacked intermediaries who could handle all of the legal, trust, and connectivity logistics that have prevented individuals from sharing their stuff with strangers. The value proposition of this business model includes:

- **Transaction Fees:** Entrepreneurs who facilitate sharing can earn transaction fees in the range of 3% to 50% of the fee charged by individuals to other individuals they share with.
- **Screening:** The property-sharing platform often screens people who share, so individuals who want to share can operate in a trusted environment.
- **Monetize Underutilized Assets:** The individuals who share receive a fee (that should be below a commercial rental company's fee) that they set or that you set in exchange for sharing.
- **Cost:** Renting property from another individual is usually much cheaper than renting property from a commercial business that has to cover overhead.
- **Social Responsibility:** Sharing reduces the carbon footprint of people who seek out these services (fewer cars and motorcycles are being purchased).
- **Variety:** People who choose to use these services don't have to buy the property being shared, so they can experience a variety of different cars, hotels, or other property being shared.
- **Why It's Disruptive:** It's cost-prohibitive for individuals to find, screen, and track other individuals without an online, peer-to-peer platform that does it for them.

DRAGON LORE

Peer-to-peer sharing works best for sharing insurable property that requires a large capital investment. Incorporate trust-building features into your platform, including liability insurance, screening, and payment processing.

Peer-to-peer sharing is an emerging industry that is facilitated by social media networks online. When Snap Stands visited the Dragons' Den, they came with an idea that blends an old-world business idea—the photo booth—with social media technology.

SNAP STANDS

Pitchers: Peyvand Padidar and Marc Fallows, Season 6, Episode 6

PRODUCT DESCRIPTION

A modern version of the traditional photo booth.

BACKGROUND

Peyvand and Marc did market research and found that there are no photo-taking kiosks on the market that capture email addresses and other survey data.

PROBLEM STATEMENT

It's awkward to take and share self-portraits at special events.

BUSINESS MODEL

Snap Stands is a photo-booth-rental company that provides event holders with photo-branding and user-data-collection opportunities. Event attendees can take photos and share them instantly with their friends through social networks. The company manufactures each photo-sharing kiosk for $1,600 and rents them out for $1,500 per day, including delivery and set-up.

PROOF OF CONCEPT

- **Capacity:** The company has reached technical proof of concept market-ready kiosks. The company has been in business for three months.

DRAGONS' DEAL

- **The Ask:** $15,000 for 25% equity.
- **Company Valuation:** $60,000.
- **The Deal:** $15,000 for 25% equity and the opportunity to deal with one Dragon who has experience helping everyday people grow their investments.

START-UP ESSENTIALS: Peer-to-Peer Sharing Business Model

1. Choose a **property type** to be shared.
2. Establish **sharing rules and policies** such as return policies, transaction fees, and pick-up and drop-off logistics.

3. License a white-label **platform** or build your own to facilitate online property sharing.

4. Set up an online **payment-processing platform** such as PayPal, Square Canada, or WebPay.

5. **Beta test** your solution with non-paying users including family, friends, and colleagues to test your model. Have them actually share property for the test.

6. **Pilot test** your solution with paying customers in a small geographic area to establish a critical mass of sharers, and to work out kinks in your platform.

7. Use a **region-by-region rollout**, so you can establish a critical mass of "sharers."

8. Get the word out through your own **social networks**, and those of your family and friends.

PART V SELF-STUDY WORKSHOP

Crowdsourcing is as scalable a business model as any business model out there. The strength of being an online intermediary, who facilitates the crowdsourcing process, is that your business can grow quickly through the use of technology. In this workshop, describe how your business model is scalable.

BUILD A SCALABLE BUSINESS

1. Set up a **note-taking system** on your computer or in a notebook to track the steps.

2. Break down your **method of producing your product or performing your service** into 7 to 10 steps, as if you were telling someone else how to do it.

3. Revise and refine your notes over time into **a cookbook** of sorts, complete with the supplies required, the inputs involved, and the detailed micro-steps involved for each stage.

4. List **at least three suppliers** for every raw material used in the production of your product or delivery of your service.

5. Describe your process for acquiring **new staff** on short notice:
   - ❏ Temp agencies
   - ❏ Staffing firms
   - ❏ Headhunters
   - ❏ Other

6. What part of your product or service offering is **standardized?**

7. What part of your product or service offering is **consumable?**

- ❑ Product or service itself
- ❑ Service agreements
- ❑ Planned obsolescence (will need to be replaced in the future)
- ❑ Other

In this chapter, we discussed how underutilized assets are being put to work and monetized because of a connected economy. The car you are not using all the time can now be shared and monetized with strangers who have short-term requirements. The vacation property you enjoy once or twice a year can now be shared with strangers who are willing to rent it from you. The extra office space that you wish you didn't have anymore can now be paid for by a hungry entrepreneur who needs a space two or three days a week. In the next chapter, we will discuss what to do if all else fails—you can start giving your products or services away using the freemium business model.

Part VI

If All Else Fails

If no other business model seems to fit your needs, then you can try one last model—the freemium business model, a model where giving your product or service away can lead to big profits.

CHAPTER 18

THE FREEMIUM BUSINESS MODEL

"Now the challenge is no one's ever heard of this … or its benefits or anything so you're at the bottom floor of a long, long journey."

—Dragon to Pitcher

FREEMIUM BUSINESS MODEL

Release a basic version of your web application. Track usage and iterate your solution over time based on user feedback. Offer premium paid features to free users who require increased capacity or functionality.

There is nothing new about product sampling. In the 1800s, soap makers used to give out free samples of soap to patrons to convince them to buy their products. In the 1940s, Estée Lauder could be seen at Saks Fifth Avenue giving away samples of her beauty products. Shoppers Drug Mart even figured out a way to sell product samples to students, with their $10 value packs containing razors, shampoo, toothpaste, and other sample products from a variety of vendors.

The fact is that product sampling works to encourage sales, and the Internet age is making businesses even more creative. Kellogg's uses pop-up retail outlets where people who agree to tweet a Kellogg's branding message at their TweetShop receive free product samples in exchange. Atlanta Bread Company gives out free cookies to anyone who likes them on Facebook. Kleenex lets us gift product samples to our friends just by entering their addresses on a webpage form. And of course we all love the daily free endless Costco food samples that trigger impulse buys in-store.

But what's missing from traditional product sampling is **customer lock-in.** If you give someone a free product sample, what's to stop them from buying from a competitor? Even if they enjoyed your free sample, they still haven't made a long-term commitment to using your product. There is no penalty to them if they buy from someone else. That's where **freemium** comes in. Freemium is a business model where you offer a basic free version of your service to customers. The cost of free to you should be negligible, so it works for software online, not free gold. Once the customer invests substantial time using your service, the cost to switch to a different service becomes enough of a hassle that the customer stays with your service. At this point, you can start selling premium features to that customer to enhance their experience with your product— including increased upload capacity, high-priority service, and other features.

Most business models are iterated over time as you start incorporating feedback from customers, investors, and other stakeholders. When Rohan Mahimker and Alexander Peters visited the Dragons' Den, they had a beta-tested product, a clear market, and a plan for making money—a $30-a-month subscription fee for access to their online educational math program. But one Dragon in particular, with deep experience in the educational software market, shot the revenue model down immediately. His argument was that there is a lot of free educational software online, so why would anyone pay for a monthly subscription? While the Dragons weren't impressed with this business plan and Mahimker and Peters left without a deal, the pitchers learned from the experience, and, after being on the show, the company started offering a freemium model with basic free access to over 250 math skills, and the opportunity to pay for premium features through a monthly, lifetime, or annual fee.[1]

SMARTEACHER

Pitchers: Alexander Peters and Rohan Mahimker, Season 7, Episode 6

PRODUCT DESCRIPTION

SMARTeacher is an online game that teaches kids math. The game tracks emotional responses of the child during the game so it can adjust to the learning pace of each child.

BACKGROUND

Rohan Mahimker and Alexander Peters are engineering students who set out to address a need in the educational market for an online math program that adjusts to children's emotions, as well as their performance.

PROBLEM STATEMENT

When you teach children, you need to respond to their emotions so you can modify your teaching approach if a child is bored, frustrated, or disengaged.

BUSINESS MODEL

The SMARTeacher team plans on selling monthly $30 subscriptions to parents for an online educational software game that teaches math and modifies the teaching rate based on the child's emotional response to the game. The child's emotions are tracked using an electronic wrist band that the child wears.

PROOF OF CONCEPT

- **Revenue:** $0 in sales so far because the company is pre-revenue.
- **Distribution:** In talks with a potential distributor in India that has 30 schools.
- **Demand:** 150 kids tested the software and over 75% of kids played the game at home on a voluntary basis.

DRAGONS' DEAL

- **The Ask:** $120,000 for 12% equity.
- **Company Valuation:** $1,000,000.
- **The Deal:** $0. They turned down a deal for $120,000 for 50% of the company after consulting with their adviser in the Dark room.

THE WARM-UP: FREEMIUM BUSINESS MODEL DEFINED

A **freemium** is a basic version of what you do best, offered free to everybody, with no requirement on your customer to pay—unless that customer requests access to your paid premium features. The reason freemium business models are so popular is because start-up businesses that sell on-demand software can use the strategy to create customer lock-in. Once a customer becomes addicted to using your service, not only does it become time-consuming to switch to another service, they might even feel compelled to pay for premium features. The key issues to consider when evaluating whether a freemium business model is right for you are:

- **Revenue Model:** You create a suite of software and services that are delivered online (i.e., software as a service) so that the incremental cost to you for each unit sold is negligible. Then you offer a basic fully functional version for free for an unlimited term, with an option to purchase premium features for a fee.
- **Product/Market Focus:** This model works particularly well for online services that require more storage or upload capacity the more dependent the user becomes.
- **Value Proposition:** The user gets to experience the software and commit to using it, without any obligation to pay for increased capacity and premium features. To succeed, the non-paying customer has to experience real value on an ongoing basis from the basic free version, not a limited-time-only basis.

Revenue Model: How to Make Money

You don't actually start a freemium business. Instead, you apply the freemium business model to a business that already exists, as a way of gaining traction in a market space. The rationale behind this business model is that consumers love free. Of course, giving away free products or services is not good for business if you don't have a plan in mind.

Here's how it works: You offer a basic version of your product or service for free, so consumers or users become dependent on it or "locked-in." Then when they need higher capacity or premium functionality, a small percentage of those consumers will convert into paying customers. Freemium works best with software online, where you offer your online service users a basic service for free, with no time limit, to all who sign up. Then you make premium features available to every one of those free users who is willing to pay a small service fee. Once hardcore users become used to using your basic free version, some of them will start demanding premium features. You make money when that small percentage of free users convert from your entry-level free version to a paid version. If you're the CEO of Dropbox and your customer runs out of space in her free account, then you allow that free customer to pay a premium for more space. If you're the head of Wix and your free customer wants access to premium design features for their free website, then you offer those features for a premium. If you're in charge of WordPress's revenue and your free bloggers request more blog space, then you offer that excess blog space for a premium fee.

Remember, this is not a free product sample at Costco … not unless Costco sets up tables and starts letting us feed freely from their refrigerators in hopes of us buying some less-accessible premium food behind the scenes. Freemium is a business strategy for creating habitual users, some of whom might convert to be consumers of your paid features. Once you achieve a critical mass of users, you can either continue your free service or shut down the freemium portion of your business to all new users.

Product/Market Focus: What Sells

So does freemium work? Can giving away a fully functional version of your on-demand software lead to real profits? Well Dropbox has raised $257 million in venture capital so far, according to Crunchbase, with freemium as a core part of its business strategy. And CEO Drew Houston says it is profitable.[2] Evernote has raised $251 million with freemium at the core of its business model, and its CEO says it is making money. And even the king of free, Facebook, is now allowing you to send real-world gifts, such as birthday chocolate, to Facebook friends. You don't even need to know your friend's address, so your friend's true privacy is maintained.

The key differentiator for this type of business model is the functionality of the online-software-as-a-service. Keep in mind that simply giving something away, in hopes that people will pay you for a premium version, is a risky approach (would you pay for Gmail or Hotmail?). Entrepreneurs who succeed using this model focus on capacity-based online platforms where continued usage leads to higher switching costs and the need for more capacity or functionality. To help you come up with your own freemium business model, consider some of the more popular product/market themes:

Freemium Theme	Description
Online Data Storage	Companies like Dropbox provide a base level of storage for free and provide users with increased storage capacity for a monthly fee per GB.
Online Note Taking	Companies like Evernote provide a basic level of storage space for free and provide users with increased uploading capacity for a small monthly fee like $5 or $10 per month.
Online Music Streaming	Companies like Spotify provide a free version and give users the capacity to access their bookmarked music anywhere for a monthly fee like $10.
Online Games	Companies like SMARTeacher provide a free version of an online game and provide users with the capacity to play at higher levels of the game for a fee.
Online Email Marketing	Companies like MailChimp provide a free version and provide users with the capacity to increase the number of users they can market to, for a monthly fee.

Freemium models work best when customers receive a set amount of free capacity and then have to pay for expanded capacity as their needs change. That capacity can be in the form of storage space, sharing ability, or contacts allowed. Focus on giving away a base level of your service that will lead to expanding needs when more users engage with your solution. If this doesn't happen, there will be no compelling *need* to upgrade to your premium features ever—unless the user *wants* to. For example, if you use a freemium model for your contact management application online, then give away X number of contacts for free, but offer a paid version for increasing needs.

Value Proposition: Why It Works

On-demand software applications are popular because they provide users with an extraordinary amount of functionality at no cost. But more importantly, the more you use them, the more dependent you become on them, so you are less likely to switch. Your usage of them creates an investment of time and data, which makes you less likely to switch from them—and as an entrepreneur you can capitalize on that lock-in aspect of software as a way to entice users to pay for premium features. The value proposition of this business model includes:

- **Free Functional Software:** As opposed to a temporary free sampling program, freemium gives users a fully functional basic version of an online platform for free. If your users like the solution, they can upgrade to premium features such as increased capacity.

- **Customer Lock-In:** When users use a free online application, they start to build a data relationship with the application. They store their photos on it, they build to-do lists, and they track their history. The last thing the customer wants to do is lose any of that history by switching to a different application.
- **Referral Engine:** Free users who never intend to quit your service or pay for premium features, once they have reached free's capacity, can be a rich source of referrals. So provide them with simple ways to invite their network to adopt your service.
- **Transition Model:** The freemium business model is a revenue model and marketing solution designed to attract customers for a broader business model.
- **Premium Features:** Fee-based features are available to those users who want trackable history, expanded storage, or removal of ads from a free version.
- **Why It's Disruptive:** People are used to receiving free versions of software, but most free software comes with limited functionality. True freemium services provide fully functional versions of their applications.

DRAGON LORE

The key to a freemium business model is to apply it to software-as-a-service businesses where user-capacity needs increase over time. The more the user engages a fully functional stripped-down version of your application, the more history he builds into the application. At some point the user will need increased capacity.

START-UP ESSENTIALS: Freemium Business Model

1. Design and develop a **free, basic, fully functional version** of your software solution.
2. **Beta test** your solution and **elicit feedback** from users to elicit new ideas for premium features that users would be willing to pay you for.
3. Design and develop **premium features** that a percentage of your free users would be willing to pay you for.
4. Set up an online **payment-processing platform** such as PayPal or Square.
5. **Launch** your service.

PART VI SELF-STUDY WORKSHOP

By now you should have a clear picture of your business model. So now it's time to prove it. Over the next 12 weeks, try to launch your new business model or re-launch your current business using the action items in this workshop.

PROVE THAT YOUR BUSINESS MODEL WORKS

1. Build a **working prototype.**
   Produce a working version or mock-up of your product or service in the next 7 to 30 days. It must be a visual representation of what you plan to sell, and can be a paper prototype if necessary. Note any takeaways or observations from the process.

2. Set up a **live demo.**
   Set up a method for conducting a live demo of your product or service to show a prospective customer how it works to solve a burning problem. Note any takeaways or observations from the process.

3. Acquire **intellectual property protection.**
   Acquire a patent, trademark, copyright, domain name, or other form of intellectual property protection that shows you have something proprietary. Note any takeaways or observations from the process.

4. Hold a **pilot test.**
   Conduct a limited market test with 10 to 100 paying customers. Pilot tests help to test the logistics of your business concept so you can work out the kinks before you invest in a full-scale business plan. Note any takeaways or observations from the process.

5. Get **testimonials.**
   Get 5 to 10 written statements from users of your working prototype that indicate satisfaction with your product or service concept. Note any takeaways or observations from the process.

6. Collect **case studies.**
   Write up case studies that describe actual scenarios from real users of your product or service. Include the event that triggered interest in your product or service, the challenge or problem the customer was looking to overcome, and how your product or service was used to solve that real problem. Follow the ethical guidelines for your industry, get permission from anyone whose name you use, and keep the case studies short. Note any takeaways or observations from the process.

7. Build a **customer list.**
   Keep track of customers and prospective customers. Note any takeaways or observations from the process.

8. Get **commitment from potential employees and advisory board members** who you have on board or will bring on board once revenue milestones have been achieved.
   Note any takeaways or observations from the process. Name them.

9. Continue to build **market traction.**
   Achieve one or more revenue milestones that have been outlined in your sales projections.

10. Write a **mini–business plan.**
    Put together a 10- to 15-slide PowerPoint presentation that explains your business. Note any takeaways or observations from the process.

Freemium is not for every business, and many businesses have gone under by attempting to provide a free service in hopes of finding a business model. But it can work in cases where free usage of an online service leads to an increased demand for extra capacity and premium features or functionality. Now that you have learned about the wide array of traditional and non-traditional business models that are available to you, it's time to recap the process of designing a business model.

CONCLUSION

THE DRAGONS' DEN PLAYBOOK

TEN STEPS TO A REAL-WORLD BUSINESS MODEL

"Be ready to revise any system, scrap any method, abandon any theory, if the success of the job requires it."[1]

—Henry Ford

THE DRAGONS' DEN PLAYBOOK

Rework your business model until you have a sustainable money-making system.

As an entrepreneur, you have the opportunity to build any number of businesses around your product. That's because your product or service is the centre of your business model, but not the business itself. You'll have a business only when you have found a market, a revenue model, and a way of packaging your product or service that generates repeat revenue. And that revenue must be enough to sustain your salary and the profit needs of the business. Without all of these factors in place *your product or service is not a business,* and you may have to license your idea to someone else who has one.

In other words, you need a business model. For example, if you want to sell chocolate, you have to find a business model that you are capable of executing. Your business model might be to produce the raw chocolate that chocolatiers need to make their chocolate creations. That's chocolate supplier Barry Callebaut's business model. Your business model might be to turn raw chocolate into chocolate creations and then retail them through your own upscale stores. That's chocolatier Godiva's business model. Or your business model might be as a bean-to-bar manufacturer, including moulding and packaging chocolate into chocolate bars, and then distributing them through retailers. That's chocolate manufacturer Hershey's business model. Each of these businesses has what is essentially the same product (with different quality levels) at the centre of their business models. But their business models are uniquely their own because they create value, generate revenue, and have their own product/market focus.

THE DRAGONS' DEN PLAYBOOK: Ten Steps to a Real-World Business Model

STEP 1: PROTOTYPE

Create a functional and monetizable prototype of your product or service.

STEP 2: FEEDBACK LOOP

Be open to constructive criticism from early testers and potential customers, and incorporate their best ideas into your product or service offering.

STEP 3: BETA TEST

Test your product or service with a limited number of friends, family members, and colleagues to elicit feedback and ideas for valuable product or service features, suggested price levels, and marketing methods.

STEP 4: PILOT TEST

Mini-launch your product or service to a limited number of paying customers and continue to gather feedback.

STEP 5: PRODUCT/MARKET FOCUS

Create a description of the product mix and customers who have been most responsive to your product or service during your beta test and pilot test.

STEP 6: VALUE PROPOSITION

Have a clear understanding of what your product or service does, the problem it solves or market void it fills, and why it is so valuable to customers.

STEP 7: REVENUE MODEL

State your revenue sources, how you charge, why your model is scalable, and how you get paid.

STEP 8: SOFT LAUNCH

Open for business with no marketing fanfare, and work out the glitches of your operation before you hard launch your business.

STEP 9: HARD LAUNCH

Launch a full-scale marketing campaign that reflects your resources. Include online marketing, SEO, social media marketing, and whatever methods provide the highest benefit for the least cost.

STEP 10: REWORK YOUR MODEL

Be prepared to make mid-course corrections to your business model if it is not working. Refine any or all of the components of your business model until your business model meets your revenue and profit objectives.

SUMMARIZE YOUR BUSINESS MODEL

1. **Revenue Model**
    - *We make money by ...*
    - *Our sources of revenue include ...*
    - *Our model is scalable because ...*

2. **Product/Market Focus**
    - *We sell [what product or service?] to [what customers?].*

3. **Value Proposition**
    - *The most valuable features of our product/service are ...*
    - *Customers use our product because it [solves a problem/does something useful/ provides emotional or social value/is valuable for another reason].*

NEXT STEPS: STARTING AND GROWING YOUR BUSINESS

Once your business starts to generate revenue and shows signs of sustainability, it's important to make sure that you have the correct infrastructure in place to run your business. If you are ready to revise and refine your business into a business that is ready to launch, then I invite you to read the companion guide to this book, *The Dragons' Den Guide to Start and Run a Small Business.* In it you'll learn how to get your business ready to launch, including how to choose an entity type, find business opportunities, seek professional help, raise money, locate your business and hire employees, deal with customers and suppliers, and more ... all using the same workshop-driven approach that you have become accustomed to in this book.

If you enjoyed this book or want to learn more, please visit the book's website at www.JohnVyge.com.

Good luck!

APPENDIX A

Free excerpt from *The Dragons' Den Guide to Investor-Ready Business Plans*

MAKING A BUSINESS-PLAN BLUEPRINT

"Success is not a God-given right. Everybody's got kids. Everybody's made sacrifices to get up here. I raised my kids. I worked two jobs. You do what you have to do."

—Dragon to Pitcher

BUSINESS-PLAN BLUEPRINT

Define your product and business. Identify your market and your competition. Establish a sustainable business model and rapid go-to-market strategy. Develop defensible financial projections. Put a qualified team in place to execute the plan. Then write it up in the form of a well-written planning document so you can share your vision with investors, banks, and other stakeholders.

Trying to create a business plan while learning all of the terminology can be like drinking water from a firehose. You are an expert in your business, and most likely don't have time to learn about valuations, term sheets, and funding requests. But you do need to understand every decision you make, even if you've hired someone else (like a business consultant, business appraiser, or chartered accountant) to help you create the required documents. Just like your financial adviser tells you never to invest in something you don't understand, you should never enter into an investment deal that you don't understand. A bird in the hand can be worth two in the bush, so sometimes the best deal you'll find is right in front of you.

If you do end up in front of an investor who shows an interest in your business, be sure to act fast. Investors can change their minds on a whim, and a deal that appears to be on the table might disappear in a flash—as the owner of Dans un Jardin found out when he was inches away from closing a $500,000 deal with a Dragon. When the pitcher hesitated, the Dragon changed his mind.

DANS UN JARDIN

Pitcher: Martin Gagné, Season 6, Episode 15

Focus: Your Business-Plan Blueprint

"This is the first automatic vending machine for liquid laundry detergent. With this machine, you reuse your bottle. The first bottle will cost you $7.99, and your refill will cost you $6.99. You save a dollar per bottle."
　—Pitcher to Dragons

PRODUCT DESCRIPTION

A self-serve laundry detergent vending machine.

DRAGONS' DEN BY THE NUMBERS

- **The Ask:** $600,000 for 40% equity in the company.
- **Company Valuation:** $1,250,000.
- **The Deal:** $0.
- **25:** The number of bottles sold per machine per week.
- **15:** The number of seconds that it takes to refill your bottle with laundry detergent.
- **12:** The number of weeks that the pitcher's machines have been in use.
- **100:** The number of new machines the company will build if it receives investor funding.

THE WARM-UP: BUSINESS PLAN DEFINED

A **business plan** is a 10- to 40-page document that outlines your strategy for each segment of your business, including your product or service, business model, sales and marketing strategy, team, and financing. The purpose of a business plan is to:

- **Define Strategy:** To describe the tactics and the product, marketing, financial, and operational strategies that you will employ to capture a definable market.
- **Secure Funding:** To describe how you plan to achieve the financial objectives of each of the stakeholders in your business (investors, customers, founders, employees).

BUSINESS PLAN TABLE OF CONTENTS

There is no set format for a business plan, only similar talking points and categories that are used across business plan formats.

The following is a sample table of contents for a business plan. Once you complete your business plan, be prepared to customize it for banks or investors as required. Please see the chapters listed below in *The Dragons' Den Guide to Investor-Ready Business Plans* for more information.[1]

TITLE PAGE
- Company Name and Logo
- Contact Information
- Business Plan Copy Number

TABLE OF CONTENTS PAGE
EXECUTIVE SUMMARY SECTION (see *The Dragons' Den Guide to Investor-Ready Business Plans* Chapter 8)

1. **VISION, MISSION, GOALS SECTION** (see Chapter 11)
   A. Business Description
   B. Vision and Mission
   C. Business Objectives
   D. Milestones
   E. Business History

2. **PRODUCT/SERVICE DESCRIPTION SECTION** (see Chapter 12)
   A. Customer Problem
   B. Product/Service Description

    C. Core Features and Benefits

    D. Proprietary Assets

    E. Product Lifecycle

    F. Product Roadmap

3. MARKET DEFINITION SECTION (see Chapter 13)

    A. Market Opportunity

    B. Target-Market Profile

    C. Growth Strategy

4. COMPETITIVE ANALYSIS SECTION (see Chapter 14)

    A. Competition

    B. Competitive Advantage

    C. Barriers to Entry

5. BUSINESS MODEL SECTION (see Chapter 15)

    A. Value Chain

    B. Product/Market Fit

    C. Revenue Model

    D. Scalability

6. SALES AND MARKETING STRATEGY SECTION (see Chapter 16)

    A. Positioning

    B. Pricing Strategy

    C. Sales Strategy

    D. Marketing Strategy

    E. Strategic Relationships

    F. Sales Forecast

7. MANAGEMENT AND ORGANIZATION SECTION (see Chapter 17)

    A. Business Organization

    B. Management Team

C. Advisory Board
D. Professional Support
E. Hiring Needs

8. **FINANCIAL PLAN SECTION** (see Chapter 18)
A. Financial Summary
B. Financing Details
C. Financial Performance
D. Risk and Mitigation

SUPPORTING DOCUMENTS
In addition to a core business plan document, a bank or investor might ask you for some or all of the following supporting documents:

- Monthly profit and loss statement, cash-flow statement, balance sheet
- Manager bios or resumés
- Legal documents (e.g., patents, intellectual property, contracts, distribution agreements)
- Product or service diagrams or flow charts
- Personal financial statements (upon request)
- Operations plan (see Chapter 19 to learn how to build this stand-alone document)

> **DRAGON LORE**
>
> Put more effort into the *business-planning* process than into the *business-plan-formatting* process. If you are not a writer, hire someone to format your notes into a proper business-planning document.

Back in 1996, two entrepreneurs, Larry Finnson and Chris Emery, launched an idea for a business based on a product that Chris's grandmother had made as a treat: Clodhoppers fudge-covered graham clusters. Ten years later, their Clodhoppers brand was sold to another company, Brookside, leaving the friends without a business to run. So they returned to their chocolate-making roots and came up with a completely new brand called OMG's, which they brought into the Dragons' Den. Their experience and expertise meant that they had a relatively easy time there, and secured a deal.

OMG'S CANDY

Pitchers: Larry Finnson and Chris Emery, Season 6, Episode 16

PRODUCT DESCRIPTION

Develop and sell a new product: chocolate graham wafer clusters mixed with gourmet nuts and crunchy toffee bits. The product comes in dark and milk chocolate flavours.

BACKGROUND

Larry Finnson and Chris Emery have been in the candy industry since 1996, when their famous Clodhoppers product was launched.

PROBLEM STATEMENT

How to replicate the commercial success of their first product, Clodhoppers.

BUSINESS MODEL

The business produces and markets a line of super-premium chocolate products that it sells through retailers.

PROOF OF CONCEPT

- **Revenue:** Current-year revenue is $0.
- **Distribution:** The pitchers plan to start selling through specialty retailers in year one, and transition to mainstream retailers in year two; years five to seven will entail retailing everywhere candy is sold in Canada.

DRAGONS' DEAL

- **The Ask:** $250,000 for 30% equity in the company.
- **Company Valuation:** $833,333.
- **The Deal:** $250,000 for 50% equity in the business.

SELF-STUDY WORKSHOP: Business Plan Pre-Work

Format your answers into the business plan format (see Business Plan Table of Contents) provided in this chapter, or use the format that your investor or bank requests. I invite you to buy a copy of *The Dragons' Den Guide to Investor-Ready Business Plans* to guide you through the process.

1. Your Audience: For **whom** are you creating your business?

   ❑ **Yourself, friends and family, individual investors:** Use the workshops in *The Dragons' Den Guide to Investor-Ready Business Plans* to develop your business plan talking points. Use the format in this book to produce your plan.

   ❑ **Investor groups, banks, business competitions:** Use the workshops in *The Dragons' Den Guide to Investor-Ready Business Plans* to develop your business plan talking points. Then format your plan using the template that is required by the organization.

2. How experienced are you at using a **word processor?**

   ❑ Experienced

   ❑ Not experienced (if not, find help)

3. How comfortable are you at putting together **financial statements?**

   ❑ Comfortable

   ❑ Not comfortable (if not, find help)

4. What types **of advisers** do you have access to?

   ❑ Chartered accountant (who can help you put together your financial statements)

   ❑ Business consultant (who can help you refine the business plan talking points that you have created)

   ❑ Lawyer (who can help you review the legal feasibility and regulatory requirements of your business model)

   ❑ Writer (who can help you format the business plan talking points that you have created in this book into a business plan)

In this appendix we outlined the eight core sections of a business plan. No business plan can be completed in one session, so be sure to complete and refine your strategy over time until you have a winning business plan.

APPENDIX B

Free excerpt from *The Dragons' Den Guide to Investor-Ready Business Plans*

PITCHING TO INVESTORS

"What I'd like to do is I'd like to circle [your] presentation around making money. It's very important. And I think we've got to move that ship, guide it in for the landing on the cash ... How am I going to make money?"

—Dragon to Pitcher

PITCHING TO INVESTORS

A pitch is an interactive discussion with an investor. Focus the core of your pitch on your business model and why the world is better off with your business concept than without it. State clearly how the investor is going to make money.

Almost a century ago, in 1916, an innovative entrepreneur named Clarence Saunders was looking for a way to improve the grocery-shopping experience and generate a healthy profit for his business. He launched a grocery store called the Piggly Wiggly in Memphis, Tennessee, based on a new business model called "self-service" shopping.[1] For the first time, shoppers could pick their own groceries off the shelf, instead of having a clerk do it for them. Not exactly a revolutionary idea by today's standards, but back then it was a hit out of the ballpark. Self-service shoppers no longer had to compete with other impatient customers for the attention of a harried clerk. They could shop themselves, pay *cash*, and then *carry* the groceries right out the door. Suddenly the grocery business was scalable, and was so successful that Piggly Wiggly still has over 600 stores today. The business model also inspired other retailers for decades to come.

What was unique about his business was not the products that were being sold, which were commodities, but the business model being used, which was a true innovation. The business model was so simple, yet revolutionary, that it soon made its way north to Toronto. Theodore Loblaw and J. Milton Cork launched their own version of the self-service grocery-shopping business model in Toronto in 1919, and called it Loblaws. And 43 years later, Murray Koffler used the self-service concept to revolutionize the drugstore industry, founding Shoppers Drug Mart in 1962. In fact, so many other businesses followed suit that self-service shopping is now the standard way to shop for groceries, pharmaceuticals, hardware, and most other retail categories. Unless, of course, you shop at Amazon, which, in its way, reverts us to the old process.

If Clarence Saunders were pitching to investors today, he would have a straightforward answer to the question that investors always ask: "What is your business model, and why is it unique?" While you might have a unique product or service, remember that investors are far more interested in your business model, and its underlying "wow" factor, than in a product or service that you think is unique. And that's what the founders of Pook Toques, a successful toque brand, had trouble convincing the Dragons of when they visited the Dragons' Den.

POOK TOQUES

Pitchers: Tony Pook and Kevin McCotter, Season 4, Episode 11

Focus: Pitching to Investors

> "We have, for the last two years, gone coast to coast at major craft shows. We were picked up by [the] Hudson's Bay Company last year. Our goal isn't just to be a toque and winter-apparel company. We want to model ourselves after the Roots store. Ideally, we want to create a Pook brand. What we've seen is a doubling in revenue each year."
> —Pitcher to Dragons

PRODUCT DESCRIPTION

Multi-functional sock hats that are made in Canada.

DRAGONS' DEN BY THE NUMBERS

- **The Ask:** $250,000 for 10% of the business.
- **Company Valuation:** $2.5 million.

- **The Deal:** $0.
- **$400,000:** Sales last year.
- **$20:** The approximate retail price of the toques.
- **$250,000:** The investment capital that the two entrepreneurs turned down from a Dragon seeking 50% equity.

THE WARM-UP: PITCHING DEFINED

A **pitch** is a verbal, visual, or written presentation that describes how you plan to employ your marketing, financial, and team resources to capture a definable market with a profitable product or service. In other words, it's a funding request you make to an investor. The purpose of a pitch is to describe your business model in a way that attracts investment capital from an investor. The following are the elements involved in pitching to an investor:

- **Pitching Formats:** Including the elevator pitch, PowerPoint pitch, executive summary, and business plan.
- **Pitching Guidelines:** Simple rules to follow to keep your pitch on track.
- **Customizing Your Pitch:** Pitch formats are not one-size-fits-all. Many active investors request that you follow their specific requirements. Some investor groups may even request that you fill out an application first. Just be flexible and willing to modify your pitching documents if an investor asks you for a particular format.

Pitching Formats

There are many ways to pitch a business. A pitch can be written, verbal, visual, or a combination of the three. The pitching format you use at any particular time depends on what stage of the investor-courting process you are at. If you have just been introduced to an investor or investor group, then a written executive summary may be requested of you, so that the investor can pre-screen your idea before you meet face to face. If you have been asked to present your pitch in person for the first time during the pre-screening phase, then a verbal elevator pitch with no visual aids may be requested. If you have passed the pre-screening phase, then you may be asked to make a formal PowerPoint presentation to an investor or group of investors so that they can see more numbers. And, finally, if your business has successfully navigated the screening process and the valuation stage, then a detailed business plan will be requested, so that that the investor can confirm that you have worked through all of the details of your venture. Each pitching format has its advantages.

PITCHING FORMATS

Elevator Pitch	PowerPoint Slide Deck	Executive Summary	Business Plan
Informal verbal presentation. Pre-screen presentation to investors. **Length:** 10 to 15 minutes, including Q&A.	Formal verbal and visual presentation. Screening session. **Length:** 15 minutes, including Q&A.	Part of an initial request or application to formally present to an investor or investor group. **Length:** 2 to 3 pages at most.	Detailed written plan that is heavily scrutinized during the due-diligence stage. **Length:** 10 to 40 pages.

Pitching Guidelines

Regardless of the type of pitch you are making, it will be judged both objectively and subjectively during the process. Objectively speaking, most investors are looking for the same thing—a clear path to a return on investment, with the secondary benefit of being able to get involved with entrepreneurs. Subjectively speaking, their opinion of your investment opportunity will depend on their industry background and an understanding of the sector you operate in.

While pitching to investors is not a professional speaking contest, there are some guidelines that you should keep in mind to enhance your presentation. We won't discuss specific components of each type of pitch here, but here are some high-level guidelines to keep your pitch on track:

- **Sector Fit:** When possible, learn the backgrounds of the investors you are pitching to so that you can appeal to their personal investment preferences.
- **Business Model:** Be able to clearly explain how and when your business will make money.
- **Feasibility:** Be able to clearly explain why your business concept is technically, market, and financially feasible.

- **Confidentiality:** Don't share any confidential information that you don't want going public. Active investors won't agree to maintain confidentiality, beyond professional courtesy, because of the sheer volume of pitches that they see.
- **Password-Protect Your Documents:** If you email your executive summary, PowerPoint pitch, or business plan, password-protect it and follow up with a call to give the receiver the password.
- **Be Brief, Yet Thorough:** Provide enough information to explain each talking point in your pitch. Avoid long-winded explanations that lose an investor's attention.
- **Be Realistic:** Make sure that your pitch is realistic and based on assumptions you can explain. Outlandish claims about the size of your potential market will destroy your credibility quickly. Know the facts about your market and your competition. The investors don't want to do your homework for you.
- **Expect Immediate Feedback:** Expect investors to freely interrupt your pitch as you're presenting it.
- **Don't Memorize:** Investors can and will throw you off track with impromptu questions during your presentation. Instead of memorizing your pitch, make a list of talking points and understand each point backward and forward, so you'll be able to get right back on track if an investor throws you off with an untimely question.
- **Check Your Grammar:** Have a third party screen your written or visual pitch for any typos or errors.

Customizing Your Pitch

Pitching formats are not one-size-fits-all. No two investors are alike, and while some will accept just about any format you give them, others may have an application or template for you to follow. For example, while *Dragons' Den* does not accept PowerPoint presentations, many other investors prefer this format. Active investors see and hear so many different pitches during the year that they need a way of standardizing them so they can find what they are looking for in an instant. In order to meet this need, be prepared to be flexible when it comes to restructuring your pitch.

The good news is that investors ask a predictable set of questions, so if you put in the groundwork with *The Dragons' Den Guide to Investor-Ready Business Plans*, you should have most of the components you'll need to meet any investor's format.

> ## DRAGON LORE
>
> Pitching formats include business plans, executive summaries, PowerPoint presentations, and elevator pitches. There is no one-size-fits-all approach, and different investors may each request that you fill out their application, or reformat your pitch to meet their requirements.

Anyone who is able to charge $700 for a water cooler clearly understands the concept of being an entrepreneur. The team members from AquaOvo have both the entrepreneurial mindset to disrupt a staid market and the managerial skills to implement a sound business plan. And that dual mindset led to a deal when they visited the Dragons' Den.

AQUAOVO

Pitchers: Noémie Desrochers and Vincent Purino, Season 6, Episode 20

PRODUCT DESCRIPTION

An eco-designed tap-water filter and dispenser that is an environmentally secure and stylish alternative to bottled water. The activated carbon filter in the porcelain water dispenser removes anything that tastes or smells funky from the water.

BACKGROUND

Pitcher Noémie and her brother Manuel (who wasn't present during the pitch) co-founded the company. Manuel designed the product and Noémie's husband, Vincent, is the marketing director.

PROBLEM STATEMENT

Plastic water coolers are old-fashioned, ugly, and not eco-friendly.

BUSINESS MODEL

The company charges $700 for stylish porcelain water-purification systems, and it generates repeat revenue from replacement carbon filters that work with the system. Desrochers and

Purino are looking to launch a mass-market BPA-free plastic model priced at $200 per unit. They also plan to license the product for a 7% royalty to companies in Europe and Japan.

PROOF OF CONCEPT

- **Revenue:** Current-year revenue projections of $700,000.
- **Distribution:** The company sells through retailers and directly through a website. The pitchers will license to companies in Europe and Japan.

DRAGONS' DEAL

- **The Ask:** $400,000 for 22% equity.
- **Company Valuation:** $1.82 million.
- **The Deal:** $400,000 for 35% of the company, plus a 3% royalty.

SELF-STUDY WORKSHOP: Pitching

Understand the basic guidelines for pitching to investors. Develop a basic understanding of the pitching formats available.

1. Which of the following **pitches** do you currently have in place?
   - ❏ Elevator pitch
   - ❏ PowerPoint pitch
   - ❏ Executive summary
   - ❏ Business plan
2. What **business sector** are you operating in? (Investors work in industry sectors that they understand.)
3. What part of your pitch would you like to keep **confidential?**
4. What proof do you have that your business plan is **realistic?**
5. Who can review your executive summary, PowerPoint pitch, and business plan for **grammar and typos?**

Investors look for business models, not just innovative products and services. They need to know how you plan to make money, so that they can figure out how they are going to get their investment back with a healthy return. The heart of your pitch, regardless of the format you use, should clearly state what your business model is.

NOTES

CHAPTER 1

1. The 5 Whys was conceived by Sakichi Toyoda prior to his death and was used to solve problems at the Toyota Motor Company. See: Jose Rodriguez Perez, *CAPA for the FDA-Regulated Industry*, Milwaukee, WI: ASQ Quality Press, 2010.

CHAPTER 5

1. Now called "Rise & Hang Travel Gear." See: "Rise & Hang Travel Gear Faces Off Against the Dragons," Rise & Hang Travel Gear, October 26, 2012, accessed January 27, 2013, http://riseandhang.myshopify.com/blogs/news/6790914-rise-hang-travel-gear-faces-off-against-the-dragons.

CHAPTER 6

1. The product was licensed through Seven Towns Limited. See: "The History of Rubik's," Rubik's official website, accessed January 27, 2013, http://www.rubiks.com/world/history.php.

CHAPTER 7

1. "The International Franchise Association," The International Franchise Association, accessed January 27, 2013, http://franchise.org/franchiseesecondary.aspx?id=526252.
2. Ibid.

CHAPTER 8

1. See 2:00 mark: nomi beo (user), "Dragons' Den Canada Season 7 Episode 7," YouTube, accessed January 27, 2013, http://www.youtube.com/watch?v=_YWP8yvyV_I.

CHAPTER 9

1. Canada's Medicinal Marijuana Store is now called "MedMe": "MedMe: Canada's Medical Marihuana Provider," MedMe, accessed January 27, 2013, http://www.medme.ca.

CHAPTER 10

1. Watch *Ludo Bites America* online: "Latest Videos," Sundance Channel / Ludo Bites America, accessed January 27, 2013, http://www.sundancechannel.com/ludo-bites-america/videos.
2. "Boxpark Shoreditch Pop-Up Mall," Boxpark Shoreditch, accessed January 27, 2013, http://www.boxpark.co.uk.

CHAPTER 12

1. "Birchbox," Crunchbase Profiles, accessed January 27, 2013, http://www.crunchbase.com /company/birchbox.

CHAPTER 13

1. Pitcher called it a community at the 20-minute mark of *Dragons' Den* Season 5, Episode 6.
2. "Company Overview," Care2, accessed January 27, 2013, http://www.care2.com /aboutus/overview.html.
3. "ReverbNation Raises $3.6 Million," newsobserver.com, accessed January 27, 2013, http://www.newsobserver.com/2012/06/22/2153715/reverbnation-raises-36-million.html.

CHAPTER 14

1. "A Potted History of Woolworths Stores," Woolworths, accessed January 27, 2013, http://www.woolworthsmuseum.co.uk/WoolworthsHistory.pdf.
2. "Our Background," vente-privee.com, accessed January 27, 2013, http://pressroom .vente-privee.com/en-GB/History.aspx.
3. Alastair Barr, "Gilt to Be Profitable This Year, Eyes IPO in 2013," *Reuters,* September 20, 2012, accessed January 27, 2013, http://www.reuters.com/article/2012/09/20 /us-gilt-ipo-idusbre88j1hl20120920.
4. Spencer E. Ante, "Are Flash Sales Still 'Fab'ulous?" *Wall Street Journal,* July 19, 2012, accessed January 27, 2013, http://online.wsj.com/article/SB100008723963904440979045 77535323312754532.html.

CHAPTER 15

1. Jeff Howe, *Crowdsourcing: Why the Power of the Crowd Is Driving the Future of Business*, New York: Crown Business, 2009.
2. Dan Primack, "Why 99designs Raised $35 Million from Accel Partners," *CNN Money*, April 28, 2011, accessed January 27, 2013, http://finance.fortune.cnn.com/2011/04/28/why-99designs-raised-3-million-from-accel-partners.
3. "Poptent (Poptent) on Twitter," Twitter, accessed January 27, 2013, http://www.twitter.com/poptent.

CHAPTER 16

1. See 34:15 mark: nomi beo (user), "Dragons' Den Canada Season 7 Episode 6," YouTube, accessed January 27, 2013, http://www.youtube.com/watch?v=Okh3LMcGZJE.
2. Securities regulators in the United States and Canada are getting involved. The United States and Canada are working on laws to determine rules for investments by non-accredited investors.
3. "Robicelli's," Indiegogo, accessed January 27, 2013, http://www.indiegogo.com/Robicellis-1.
4. Rob Lewis, "The First Pitch to Close All Five Dragons in the Den Turns to Crowdfunding," Techvibes, April 4, 2012, accessed January 27, 2012, http://www.techvibes.com/blog/the-first-pitch-to-close-all-five-dragons-in-the-den-turns-to-crowdfunding-2012-04-04.

CHAPTER 17

1. "About Hertz," Hertz, accessed January 27, 2013, https://www.hertz.com/rentacar/abouthertz/index.jsp?targetPage=CorporateProfile.jsp&c=aboutHertzHistoryView.
2. "RelayRides," CrunchBase, accessed January 26, 2013, http://www.crunchbase.com/company/relayrides.

CHAPTER 18

1. "SMARTeacher," SMARTeacher, accessed January 27, 2013, http://www.smarteacher.ca.
2. Victoria Barret, "Dropbox: The Inside Story of Tech's Hottest Startup," *Forbes*, November 7, 2011, accessed January 27, 2013, http://www.forbes.com/sites/victoriabarret/2011/10/18/dropbox-the-inside-story-of-techs-hottest-startup.

CONCLUSION

1. "Henry Ford Quotations," The Henry Ford Museum, accessed January 27, 2013, http://www.thehenryford.org/research/henryFordQuotes.aspx.

APPENDIX A

1. John Vyge, *The Dragons' Den Guide to Investor-Ready Business Plans,* Etobicoke, ON: John Wiley & Sons Canada, Ltd., 2013.

APPENDIX B

1. "About Us," Piggly Wiggly, accessed July 14, 2012, http://www.pigglywiggly.com/about-us.

Glossary

Automated Retail A modern version of a vending machine that's able to print books, sell electronics, or sell other items you wouldn't expect to see in an all-in-one vending machine.

Below-Market Fee A fee below what a commercial business would charge.

Bounty A fee that freelancers compete for in an open forum by completing measurable tasks or projects such as logo design.

Business Model A sustainable money-making system that describes what you sell, the customers you serve, and your repeat revenue.

Business Owner Someone who owns an entity that delivers products or services to a predictable stream of customers in a profitable manner.

Cloud Server space online where software-as-a-service applications and data are hosted.

Compliance When you ensure that your business meets all applicable laws and regulations.

Crowdfunding A series of individual fundraisers held by anyone, using an online platform such as Kickstarter.

Crowdsourcing A model where a number of remote individuals help complete a task that is posted online.

Deliverable The tangible or intangible outcome of a task or a project (e.g., a logo, a video, a data map).

Direct Selling Selling products through party plans or multi-level marketing.

Donor An individual who makes an online donation to an individual fundraising campaign through an online crowdfunding website (or otherwise).

Flash Sale A time-limited sale for off-price merchandise.

Franchise Disclosure Document Contains the franchisee agreement, franchise fees, franchisee capital requirements, financing options, approved supply chain, site selection criteria, training and support, system coverage, financial performance history, and other disclosures.

Freemium A free basic service that offers paid features for the free users who are willing to pay for more functionality.

Fundraiser An individual who pays a crowdfunding business a transaction fee in exchange for being given the tools to build a fundraising webpage in minutes.

Halo Effect The validation your product gets when an established retailer or intermediary decides to carry your product.

Keystone Pricing A dead-simple pricing strategy where you double the price of your whole-sale cost to establish your retail prices. Most retailers modify traditional keystone pricing by adding or subtracting a percentage based on the industry norms of your product category.

Licensee The individual or entity who pays the inventor a royalty in exchange for permission to commercialize the product of the inventor.

Licensor The inventor who allows a company or individual to commercialize his or her product.

Location-Agnostic When the customer can place an order from anywhere they happen to be using any technology they happen to have. It doesn't matter where the customer makes a purchase or picks it up. What's relevant is that the customer is allowed to make the purchase through the Web via a smartphone, or in the store, and get the same price, and then pick it up at a local retailer or ship it from a local retailer for same-day delivery.

Lock-In A customer-retention milestone when a customer has put so much effort into add-ing data to your application that he or she would not readily switch to a competitor's prod-uct. For example, if you have used Hotmail since 1995, you would incur a high switching cost to change to Gmail.

Market Traction The stage you reach in your business when you have a sustainable way of attracting paying customers.

Monetize To generate revenue from something that previously wasn't earning revenue.

Off-Price Merchandise Merchandise that is acquired at deep discount below wholesale cost.

Omni-Channel A retail strategy that employs consistent pricing, shipping, and availability of merchandise across every sales channel including smartphones, websites, and brick-and-mortar outlets.

Opportunistic Buying Buying inventory from wholesalers and manufacturers who need to liquidate their end-of-season and overstock items.

Pack-and-Hold Merchandise that is finished, packed, and ready for shipment, but is being held by the seller pending receipt of the buyer's shipping instructions.

Party-Plan Company A company that sells a themed product line through independent sales reps who hold in-home sales events.

Peer-to-Peer A connection between two individuals who each have a computer and are connected online.

Peer-to-Peer Interaction An online connection between two members of an online community.

Peer-to-Peer Transaction A transaction over the Internet, between two individuals who may or may not be in business.

Performance Standards Minimum sales guarantees that a licensor requests from the licensee in exchange for licensing rights.

Platform A sophisticated web application that automatically performs the online functions of your business, and includes an interface and back-end software.

Pop-Up Retail A business that has no permanent location that opens up in a physical retail outlet for a short period of time to capitalize on season sales, to test a concept, or to penetrate a new market.

Pre-Revenue The business stage when you have a business concept and a prototype, but you have not started generating revenue yet.

Private Label Putting your brand name on someone else's product with permission from the manufacturer.

Product Developer A person who develops a tangible product that can be licensed or sold directly to distributors or consumers.

Product Placement A process where a company pays to be included in a sample product-of-the-month subscription box club. But most subscription services don't charge manufacturers for placement in their boxes in order to maintain their objectivity.

Pyramid Scheme An illegal practice where independent sales reps get paid to recruit and sell starter kits to new sales reps, with no material business of buying and selling actual products taking place by any of the sales reps.

Revenue Model Your sources of revenue and how you charge for your product or service.

Royalty An upfront or ongoing percentage or dollar payment to an inventor in exchange for the right to manufacture and distribute an invention.

Scale The ability to grow your business operation without putting excess stress on your financial and human resources.

Sell Sheet A one-page marketing piece used by an inventor to secure a licensing agreement. It includes an image of the invention, features, attributes, benefits, and a call-to-action of what the inventor would like the potential licensee to do next.

Sell-Through The amount of your inventory that is sold by retailers.

SEO An acronym for search engine optimization, which improves the search engine ranking of a website through the creative use of keywords, backlinks, and website domain names.

Showrooming A situation where customers browse bricks-and-mortar retail outlets to gain an understanding or appreciation of a product's quality and features, and then search online for the cheapest buying opportunity.

Smell Test Looking for obvious signs such that your business may or may not work (e.g., revenue to date).

Soft Launch Pre-launching your business with no marketing to a small group of people.

Software as a Service Also known as SaaS, software as a service describes a software application hosted in the cloud, so you don't necessarily have to install it on your local computer if you don't want to.

Turnkey Business A business that can be up and running quickly, because the operating model is already proven, documented, and set up for you.

Upsell To sell an add-on product or service to someone who is already a paying customer.

Use Case A list of steps that a user or consumer of your invention would follow to achieve the intended result of the invention.

User-Generated Content Website content that is created by individuals. For example, Indiegogo contains thousands of webpages, each created by individuals who use the site to create individual fundraising campaigns.

Users People who use your software or website online.

White-Label Software A software program that can be licensed and branded by a third party for commercial purposes.

ACKNOWLEDGEMENTS

Thank you for buying this book, because the real catalyst for this book is you—an entrepreneur who has decided to take action on a business idea, with the hope of changing your life for the better. Everyone who watches *Dragons' Den* loves it—not just because it's entertaining, but because it shows every person in this country that an idea can be turned into a business that will change their life and the community around them.

There are many people who need to be thanked for putting this book together:

The team at the CBC *Dragons' Den*, including Marc Thompson, Tracey Tighe, and Karen Bauer, with specific thanks to Molly Duignan, producer of CBC *Dragons' Den* and resident expert on the show, and to Doug Burgoyne, founder of FrogBox and a participant on the show, for contributing the foreword. Thanks also go to Lisa O'Connell and Lindsay Pearl at Sony/2WayTraffic for making the project possible.

The team at Wiley, with a special call-out to Pam Vokey, production editor, and Jane Withey, developmental editor, as well as the copyeditor, Jeremy Hanson-Finger.

Several others who also need to be thanked include James Murphy, a personal development expert and executive coach at Evolution for Success, who added insight and technical value to the Self-Assessment section of this book, as well as Luc Hekman, Hugh Le Blanc, Gary Rose, Jean-Marc Poirier, Raj Ananthanpillai, David Lester, Brien Fraser, Lars Bodenheimer, and Raj Narasimhan, who provided support through the writing process.

Personal thanks go to my wife's cousin, author Marilyn Picard, for connecting me to Wiley; my entrepreneurial father-in-law, John Milne, Sr.; my mother-in-law, for her constant support and quiet strength; and my parents, John and Annette Vyge, for their support and inspiration. And, finally, my wife and partner in life, Sandy, for her support, and our two children, Trinity and Whitney, who helped me think through many of the words on these pages during our routine "monster walks" through the parks and fields around our home. Your passion for learning new things continues to inspire me every day.

ABOUT THE AUTHOR

John Vyge is a Certified Financial Planner™ professional and business plan analyst who provides 360° business plan and investor pitch assessments to start-up entrepreneurs and offers education sessions to accelerators. He researches fast-growth companies to develop insight for his recommendations. John is the author of *The Dragons' Den Guide to Assessing Your Business Concept, The Dragons' Den Guide to Investor-Ready Business Plans,* and *Model Marketing Kit,* a contributing author for *Investing in an Uncertain Economy For Dummies,* and was a technical reviewer for *76 Tips for Investing in an Uncertain Economy For Canadians For Dummies.* He has been quoted in various publications including the *Washington Post, Business Week* online, *Investment News Magazine,* BankRate.com, and *Insurance & Advisor* magazine.

INDEX

Looking for More?

Visit www.JohnVyge.com

Talk to the Author Online
Share Your Brand Story
Download Worksheets
and more …

Bring these concepts into your business through training initiatives,
consulting engagements, and keynote addresses.